DAD... IN AMERICA WE HAVE BASEMENTS, IN AU
SHEDS! I PICKED UP THIS BOOK & OPEN
PAGE 17 AND IT REMINDED ME OF GRAn
FRONT OF HIS GARAGE AT THE END OF
AS YOU CONTINUE TO SORT THROUGH GRANDPAS UNDERGROUND
SHRINE, MAYBE YOU CAN LOOK THROUGH THIS BOOK ONCE IN
AWHILE — THERE ARE LOTS OF SIMILARITIES. ENJOY — HOPE-
FULLY ONE DAY YOU WILL GET TO SEE A REAL LIFE
"AUSSIE" SHED IN PERSON.
MERRY CHRISTMAS
DAD!

THE COMPLETE
BLOKES&SHEDS

now including **STORIES FROM THE SHED**

LOVE —

AUSTRALASIAN INSTITUTE OF BACKYARD STUDIES

A higher purpose.

THE COMPLETE BLOKES&SHEDS

now including STORIES FROM THE SHED

MARK THOMSON

Angus&Robertson

An imprint of HarperCollins*Publishers*

Angus&Robertson

An imprint of HarperCollins*Publishers*, Australia

Blokes & Sheds first published in Australia in 1995
Stories From the Shed first published in Australia in 1996
This combined edition first published in Australia in 2002
by HarperCollins*Publishers* Pty Limited
ABN 36 009 913 517
A member of the HarperCollins*Publishers* (Australia) Pty Limited Group
www.harpercollins.com.au

HarperCollins*Publishers*
25 Ryde Road, Pymble, Sydney NSW 2073, Australia
31 View Road, Glenfield, Auckland 10, New Zealand
77–85 Fulham Palace Road, London W6 8JB, United Kingdom
Hazelton Lanes, 55 Avenue Road, Suite 2900, Toronto, Ontario M5R 3L2
and 1995 Markham Road, Scarborough, Ontario M1B 5M8, Canada
10 East 53rd Street, New York NY 10032, USA

National Library of Australia Cataloguing-in-Publication data:

Thomson, Mark, 1955–.
Blokes & sheds: now including Stories from the shed.
ISBN 0 207 19823 3.
1. Men – Australia – Social life and customs – Anecdotes. 2. Toolsheds – Social aspects – Australia – Anecdotes. 3. Australia – Social
life and customs – Anecdotes. I. Title. II. Title: Blokes and sheds. III. Title: Stories from the shed.
392.36

Cover photograph by Mark Thomson. All photographs shot on Olympus cameras
Printed in China by Everbest Printing Co. on 115gsm Korean Matt Artpapers
5 4 3 2 1   02 03 04 05

Contents

Blokes & Sheds

Stories from the Shed

Acknowledgements

For their assistance and inspiration, my thanks to: Dave Glazbrook, Leon Earle, Eric Algra, Jennifer Layther, Annabelle Collett, Tony and Terry from Yodel Action, Helen Fuller, Michael Lee, Dave Whyte, John Schumann, Les Lloyd, Francesco Barbaro, Tubby Justice and, especially, my daughter Billie, who enjoys hammering nails into timber offcuts.

My special thanks to the hundreds of shed owners who allowed me inside their sheds and shared their thoughts with me.

All photographs were shot with an Olympus OM2 using a 28 mm lens on Ilford FP4 rated at 125 ASA, using existing light. My thanks to Deborah Workman for her care and commitment in the darkroom.

The author's shed

Mark has seen a lot of sheds. When he came across this one a few years ago, he knew just how to fit it out. He's pretty pleased with the result; his only complaint is that it's too small.

Working from home with a computer, Mark likes to go to his shed every day for a break. It doesn't matter what he does there — whack a piece of wood, rearrange things or generally muck around — the thing is that he's doing something with his hands.

Mark looks forward to his shed mellowing over the years.

BLOKES&SHEDS

"You can do anything in a shed" — Gary

Now there's a good shed . . .

Sheds are an integral part of Australian life. No other nation values them as we do. Despite this, our sheds, modest from the outside yet glorious on the inside, have never really been recorded or their many purposes explained. Sheds come and go with no-one the wiser, remaining secret and mysterious places that are exposed only at a garage sale or on the death of their owners. The purpose of this book is to throw some light on why the backyard shed sustains life and meaning for so many men.

In a shed the rules are different. Here, chaos is allowed to reign, asserting its creative force in wayward contrast to the suburban order all around. It's a place that permits the presence of spiders, sawdust and stinks. The acrid smell of gardening chemicals mixes with the reek of damp, mould and old oil; light softened through dusty windows never gets to the murky corners. Danger lurks. Hidden in rough painted cupboards are forbidden chemicals. Rusting nails lie scattered around the floor, ready to pierce unprotected feet. Screeching power tools send sparks flying. Risks and thrills are everywhere.

Old biscuit tins and Vegemite jars full of nails, screws and washers await the pleasure of being sorted and reused. Tobacco tins bursting with bits of wire, broken plugs, old glasses and pieces of machined steel — clearly a part of some device only to be wondered at — squat on sagging shelves. Never throw them out. Their time will come.

A shed can be a reservoir of memories and experience, rich with satisfying layers of accumulated personal history.

Time can stand still here, making it a place for meditation and contemplation. Some men go to their sheds to escape from family responsibilities, never really to emerge again. Others make their sheds the centre of family and community life, using them as places for preparing food, brewing beer, making music, playing sports, sharing information and generally socialising.

Sheds transcend class. All sorts of people, rich and poor, city and country, are sustained by their sheds. Anyone with the modest luxury of a reasonably sized building block can construct one in their backyard.

Sheds also transcend age. Young men go to them to be initiated into the mysterious art of making a motor vehicle go or brewing beer, while retired men take advantage of the quietude to work and yet not work — an opportunity to tinker away their twilight years.

Our national knack for invention and innovation, for making do, lives on in the shed. The "she'll be right" attitude may be denigrated as the blight of Australian industry, but it thrives in the country's backyards. And it's this do-it-yourself ethos that gives the shed supremacy. A shed is a palace of practicality where a bloke is the ruler.

In this book you'll find just some of the types of sheds that grace our backyards. Like their contents, sheds come in all shapes and sizes and their purposes range the spectrum. What binds them is something undefinable, something as mysterious as the dark corners of their interiors — something that happens when a bloke gets a shed.

Definitions

In Australia a shed can be anything from a dunny-size construction to an aircraft hangar covering an acre or two. A shed might be defined as a building outside or away from the main domestic living space. However, this doesn't go far enough; a rumpus room can demonstrate shed-like qualities, even though it's part of the house. Perhaps what really makes a shed a shed is the value placed on it by its owner.

A garage is not a shed: it's simply a place in which to store a car. However a garage can, given a little care and attention, become a shed. Many of the sheds included here could also be called home workshops.

Shed, n. a rough structure or lean-to, built for shelter, storage etc.
(Medieval English shadde, Old English scead, sced shelter, shade)

In choosing sheds to include in this book, an important criterion for selection was that their owners or occupiers were men. That's not to say that women don't have sheds or other special spaces, but the link between men and sheds is a strong one. Australian blokes like their sheds and spend a lot of time in them.

Sheds are not uniquely Australian. Many countries have similar domestic spaces: America has its basements, for instance. However, in Australia the average home has plenty of space, and our standard of living is high enough to allow for the cost of spare domestic buildings.

The basic model

This hay shed, perched like a strange giant insect high on a windy hill,
says it all: a roof to keep the rain off and provide some shade.
Getting out of the weather is a good start.

Rural origins

In many a discussion about sheds you'll hear blokes talk about what a great one their grandfather, uncle or father had on the farm.

The ability to fix anything with a few basic materials and a streak of ingenuity is firmly entrenched in Australian folklore. There has been a deeply ingrained suspicion that store-bought gear, with its flashy packaging, is ultimately mere trickery, and that there's always a tool, method or shortcut that can do the job.

The grand tradition of do-it-yourself goes back to the beginning of white settlement. With transport slow and distances from cities great, an ability to solve any number of small engineering or manufacturing problems was necessary for a farmer's survival. A broken plough could not be repaired by a quick phone call or a part trucked up from the city overnight. The problem had to be fixed through ingenuity and resourcefulness.

This aptitude for nifty solutions with a length of fencing wire, a hammer and a piece of 4" x 2" timber is strongly ingrained and widely felt to be some sort of national competitive advantage. People take pride in such skills, even when more sensible solutions may be available.

While we like to evoke this tradition of backyard self-sufficiency, most people now live in the capital cities, and the majority of Australian men wouldn't know how to fix a Southern Cross windmill or tell the difference between wheat and barley. The ideal of the self-sufficient handyman nevertheless persists, manifested in the domestic shed.

Meanwhile farmers, always practical and level-headed, don't stand for this kind of sentimental mush. As farm machinery has grown a lot larger and mechanically more sophisticated, the average farm shed is now more likely to resemble a small factory or a truck-repair workshop. Heavy vehicles such as semi-trailers are now common on farms. The romantic stone or timber shed is almost a thing of the past. The practical farm shed is now more likely to be the size of a small aeroplane hangar. It's not easy to get the same character into a vast echoing steel cube.

The Stumpenschuppen

John likes old country buildings. So much so that he dismantled this one made of interlocked mallee roots and painstakingly reassembled it on his own property some distance away.

When he was finished, John invited some locals from the nearby pub to admire his handiwork. They got out of the car — and promptly fell about laughing. "You've made the walls too straight," they said.

Stumpenschuppen have surprisingly effective insulation properties, especially when the inside wall is given a coating of mud. Early farmers often built and lived in them on arrival to this country, as they could be built almost entirely from found natural materials.

Ron's implement shed

Ron and his wife Glenda live out in the Mallee on a 800-acre farm first settled by Ron's father before the First World War. This traditional implement shed was built in the 1920s and Ron can recall as a boy helping his father roof it. Using straw grown especially for the purpose, the roof was cut and laid in such a way as to keep out the rain. Even now, more than half a century on, it is still a highly functional building, with a range of tools and implements housed within it, quietly waiting to be used.

Ron and Glenda's farm comprises a number of substantial buildings, some using the distinctive white limestone and orange mortar of the area. The buildings are a testament to the labour of several generations in the marginal Mallee country.

Rusty

Rusty is a retired drover and grazier. He and his wife retired to a small
town near Tamworth after a lifetime of working on cattle stations.
Rusty spends a lot of his time in his shed, where he makes greenhide
whips for people who appreciate his skills. He still brings out his old
squeezebox now and then, playing the traditional tunes that he and
his friends have performed at country dances since his childhood.
Rusty doesn't have much time for country and western music.
"You can't play guitar on the back of a horse," he says scornfully.
"But the squeezebox you can put into a sugarbag and take anywhere."

Luxmore

Luxmore lives out on a farm with more sheds than he can be bothered counting; some are up gullies he hasn't visited in years. At least a few of them are chock full of the sort of old gear that makes inner-city antique and curio dealers drool. You know the kind of thing — an old soft-drink crate with a few wormholes which, when scrubbed up and varnished, is given an outrageous price tag as genuine Australiana. It doesn't pay to get too clever with Luxmore, though. He may wear those old Police and Fireman braces, but he knows full well that the 1964 Falcon ute with only 30,000 miles on the clock is worth a packet. That's why the locals say he's been known to shoot first and ask questions later if you go driving around his place at night. Be warned, junk dealers.

Rule 1: Never throw anything out

One tradition of the farm shed which still survives in the urban equivalent is hoarding. "You never know when you'll find a use for that" is a common excuse for the elaborate storage of vast supplies of string, timber offcuts, pieces of electrical conduit, nuts and bolts, oddly shaped (but somehow useful-looking) pieces of metal and thousands of other bits and pieces.

The most important thing to remember about stored stuff — and, in fact, about

having a shed — is not whether you actually *do* anything with all these fabulous resources; rather, it's the potential of what these things *could* be that's the exciting thing.

And when you finally do find a use for that old clock part you put away 17 years ago or that 10-year-old punctured bicycle tube, the thrill, the satisfaction, is like none other. You have shown admirable foresight, practicality and economy of resources.

Like all great wisdom, there are entirely practical and sensible reasons at the heart of the "never chuck out" tradition. The experience of the Great Depression is often invoked by older shed owners, and such memories of poverty die hard. But they're not the only people annoyed at the flagrant wastefulness of modern living. European migrants who went through the hardships of the Second World War are also highly conscious of waste. One shed owner tells of a neighbouring Hungarian couple who had kept every paper and plastic shopping bag since 1947. Their hallway was a dark tunnel lined with neatly folded and stacked bags.

There's a bit of a revival going on when it comes to hoarding and storing stuff. This is particularly so when it comes to timber, the prices for which are steadily rising around the world. Consequently there's now a whole new wave of younger shed owners who, like their fathers before them, are accumulating a satisfying collection of offcuts and breadboard-size bits of wood that look far too good to throw out. They're discovering the richness that lies within such frugality.

Keep a thing
for seven years . . .

When Ross (shown here with his son David on the left) moved down
to the city from the bush he found he had a lot of stuff to take with him.
"When you live in the bush you have to do things yourself," says Ross.
"If you do it yourself you'll also know that it's been done properly."

Ross believes that it's important to have enough things on hand to be
able to complete a job satisfactorily. "If you keep a thing for seven years,
you'll find a use for it," he explains. His shed is an organised space,
despite the appearance of vast quantities of apparently random gear.

The Depression and the war years taught Ross the importance of
having a comprehensive shed, giving rise to the notion
that it is best to buy the tool, not the article.

The return of thrift

Lee is an artist whose shed is an integral part of his work. With a view over a small, leafy garden, this naturally lit space is true shed rather than a "studio". Some of Lee's work currently involves weaving baskets and traps from creepers and vines found in suburban gardens, making useful objects from stuff that other people would simply dump in the rubbish bin. In a similar way his shed is made from bits of found timber, iron and "junk" merged into a pleasing whole.

"My shed grows organically," Lee says. "Come back in four years' time and it'll be bigger." His shed is a statement about a consumer society in which people are defined by what they buy instead of what they save.

Lee makes a subsistence living from his artwork and from gardening. Thrift is on the way back.

Tool heaven

This shed is a memorial to tools. Trevor has amassed an enormous collection of planes, saws, drills and other woodworking tools. "It started out as a hobby but it's gotten out of control," says Trevor. His pride and joy is his plane collection, with instruments ranging from a tiny violin maker's plane to a massive five-foot cooper's plane. Drawer after drawer reveals obscure and curious-looking instruments in steel and wood, often possessing an elegant functionality.

In the tradition of craftsmen passing on their tools from father to son, some of the old wooden planes have had many generations of use. The places where thumbs and fingers have grasped the tool have, over many decades, worn deep depressions in the beech patina. Even so, it's possible to trace the manufacturer's stamps from the early days of the Industrial Revolution. Many of these tools have had a history longer than white Australia's — coming to Australia in an immigrant's luggage, or having been used to make what is now valuable early colonial furniture.

Trevor hopes one day to open up his collection as a museum.
It will be a fine spot to visit.

Small beauties

Bob is one of the hidden talents that reside in Australia's sheds.
A retired toolmaker and production engineer, he makes beautiful,
scaled-down vintage cars in this very shed. Wheel hubs, cowlings, door
panels and all sorts of parts that would normally require a whole car plant
to produce are fabricated by some cleverly made tools, a lathe, ingenuity,
patience and a big store of bits and pieces. ("I'm a bit of a bowerbird,"
confesses Bob.) His cars are even driveable — a small chainsaw motor
means they can chug around the backyard very nicely.

Bob has nothing but disdain for the chequebook restorers, the yuppies
who pester him to sell one of his beautiful miniature Bentleys or Jaguars.
The more they pester him, the less likely he is to sell. What a luxury . . .

The backyard mechanics' institute

Brian's shed is a model of practical self-sufficiency and order.
Even the twine for tying up tomatoes is ranked in order of length.

The shed itself was bought second-hand, unbolted and reassembled
in Brian's backyard. The *pièce de résistance* is the small study —
the back of a pantechnicon which was removed from its chassis and
bolted onto the side of the shed. A firm floor, some old carpet and
electricity then provides the basis for a cosy little study area.

Brian believes in the virtues of self-improvement — a trade union
tradition that harks back to the days of mechanics' institutes and workers'
educational programmes. Not that Brian's shed is all given over to
such earnestness. In one corner, a piece of floral cloth hides a huge,
gleaming Ducati motorbike in immaculate condition.
Several times a month Brian dons his leathers and disappears over
the horizon, blowing out the cobwebs as the bike leans into
yet another corner at high speed . . .

In praise of disorder

Order and disorder in the domestic shed are one of the great sticking points of domestic harmony. In a home that is the very picture of good taste, organised and polished to within an inch of its life, why does the bloke insist on having this revolting festering wound of a shed?

The shed is an outbreak of dirt and chaos in what is otherwise a serenely ordered world. And therein lies the secret. If life has been reduced to a series of routines, there's a powerful need for a safety valve that allows the pressure of organisation, appearances and expectation to be released. The shed is that valve, somewhere to go a bit slack.

Why should everything in the domestic environment be totally ordered? Aren't such attitudes simply the product of reading too many home-decorating magazines? It doesn't have to be that way. As one shed owner said, "Once everything is organised you might as well be dead, because there's nothing else to do."

The creeping demand for total domestic order is, no doubt, based on sound scientific principles for exterminating all vermin and disease, but it means that there are no mysteries for kids to explore, no unplanned areas of unknown around the home in which unimaginable things may lurk. How can

Australian kids ever hope to run the clever country if they have no grasp of shed culture and the great potential that lies within bent pieces of wire and old washers? And does it mean that they'll run screaming from the first sight of a redback spider at age 27?

It's the potential of what can happen in a shed that really matters, not what actually takes place. If it's totally ordered then that potential is less likely to be realised: it's just a shed. Instead, it's far more satisfying for work to be in progress, to have limitless possibilities waiting to happen.

Of course, there's nothing really wrong with an ordered shed. Arranging possessions in a systematic way can give a shed owner a great sense of satisfaction — the joy of meeting the challenge of cataloguing so many diverse bits of stuff. It means that, finally, he can sit back and enjoy the majesty of it all spread before him.

Arguments concerning ordered versus disordered sheds will no doubt continue to be voiced for as long as sheds exist, but ultimately it's not important how your shed looks — as long as you've *got* a shed.

Personal compost

Brian has a great shed. He has collected a wondrous array of treasures and has arranged them in a witty and enjoyable way.

There's a stuffed dingo with a doll in its mouth, a brass Buddha smoking a giant pipe, a throne-like chair covered with kangaroo skin.

Here is a person who gains immense satisfaction from his shed, "turning it over," he says, "like personal compost." Brian is a shining example of the benefits of accumulation.

The feral shed

If anyone thinks that a good shed is something that only old codgers
have, then think again, because David's shed is only four years old.
It's a place for swapping bike parts and for creative experimentation
of all kinds. Bikes and sheds go hand in hand.

David collects stuff, really good stuff sometimes, from around the street.
Some of it is turned into art. He likes old stuff because it's often
more robust, enduring and easier to fix than the new, plasticky equivalent.
"I like old things because you can use them. I like the way they're made.
Old tools are more beautiful. I can't explain it . . ." Take the bicycle
he's leaning on. It weighs a ton and has one of those really hard leather seats,
but it still works. Will the same be true of a K-Mart
mountain bike in 60 years' time?

David lives at the back of his shed in a suite of tiny rooms made
out of packing crates.

Everything

Bill lives out of town on a big block of land where he has acres of stuff, some stored in sheds and some just out in paddocks. Some of the sheds are piled so high that opening the door reveals an impenetrable wall of things. There are cardboard boxes full of magazines, car parts, second-hand paint, kitchen appliances, early computers, video games, cake tins full of springs, rolls of sandpaper, vinyl toys, barbecuing tools, spark plugs (new and old), combination screwdrivers, TV products from the 1970s, chemicals, ironing-board covers and thousands of other things too numerous to name. This is a treasure trove, where everything is potentially valuable, where everything has an equal right to existence.

Bill goes to lots of clearance sales, often buying job lots in order to purchase one particular car part or object of value. He sells some of his stuff, but the rest is kept waiting for that time when it may become valuable. "Some boxes I haven't even opened yet," says Bill.

Some people don't like disorder. Bill doesn't seem to mind it.

A place where I make the rules

Australian blokes are pretty lucky, there's no doubt about it. Many of them do have a space that they can call their own — their shed. Does it mean that they're simply ducking out of their family responsibilities or are they genuinely alienated within their own homes?

Retirement, for many men, brings a realisation that the domestic space which they have shared for so many years is clearly the domain of the female

partner and that it is not easy for the patterns of a lifetime to change. "You put down a cup of coffee on a table in the house," said one shed owner, "and a moment later the wife swoops down with a dishcloth, lifts the cup up and wipes away a possible coffee ring stain. You get the message soon enough, I'll tell ya."

Social pressures have traditionally assigned women the responsibility for raising a family, a task that requires a degree of control over the whole house. Aware of this fact and the limits it puts on his freedom, a bloke craves a place of his own, a space where he can maintain his identity and maybe even repair it when necessary. Like a shed, for instance. "Somewhere I can put something down and it will still be there next week," says one shed owner.

There is a saying uttered by the wives of newly retired men which goes, "I married my husband for better or for worse but not for lunch every day." Spare a thought for the retired man banished to his shed with his lunch box at 8 am, not to return to the house until 5.30 pm.

It would be a mistake to underestimate the importance of sheds in men's lives. Many men clearly do feel a sense of powerlessness with their lot in life, and a small space of their own does not seem too much to ask. It affords them a sense of independence and autonomy while at the same time maintaining the family unit at close hand.

The shed can be a refuge from turbulent times, a constant when all around is changing.

Some men do withdraw to their sheds like a hermit crab into a shell, creating shed widows and shed orphans. Marriages and families have been known to fall apart as a result of men spending too much time in sheds. What we need is a happy medium.

Plenty of women are discovering the joys of shed-type spaces — sewing rooms are a traditional example. Increasing numbers of women are building their own sheds — but that's another book . . .

The family therapist

Dr Michael Lee, shown here on the left with his son and father, is a family therapist who takes a professional interest in the role of the shed in Australian family life. He classifies sheds in a range from benign to malignant. A benign shed, like the one shown here, is one which has no capacity to sustain life. In fact, it would probably only contain a few nasty garden chemicals. From there, the scale shifts upwards until it reaches the malignant category: a shed with many life-sustaining properties — fridge, stove, phone, computer, even a bed. Many of the sheds in this book are deeply malignant.

While Michael's analysis is light hearted, he does acknowledge that there is a disturbing side to the divisions within families about spaces and the role of men. Men do retreat to their sheds and it is often difficult to coax them back into the main framework of family life. Some, no doubt, would argue that they're completely happy where they are.

"They're lining up at the barrier for race number 8 at Randwick . . ."

Listening to the races is a time-honoured shed occupation.
Bart does not have a spectacular shed, but it is a good place to listen to the races
under the pretext of doing a job. To make the task easier, there's an old fridge;
all that tension of wondering whether your nag will come home or not
gives the shed punter a dry mouth.

There was once a time when to have a phone line from the shed to
your bookie was the height of covert punting luxury. Now, with
the development of cable TV, satellites, mobile phones, computers and the whole
information highway, the shed punter could soon become a thing of the past.

Listening to the cricket remains an ideal shed activity, however.
Even one-day cricket is sufficiently leisurely and affable to make pleasant
shed radio. Over many years, ABC cricket commentators have polished
their art to create a hazy, matey atmosphere where time does not matter and
the sleepy pace is only occasionally broken by a flurry of high-pitched
comments culminating in, "He's out!"

Small is beautiful

Murray's shed is proof that you don't need a large space to have
a successful and satisfying shed. He has lived in his inner-city house most of
his life and in the corner of his small backyard is a shed of about 2 square metres.
"Everything I need to fix anything around the house is in here," Murray
proudly says of his compact little shed. Hidden deftly in nooks and crannies are
car repair tools, serious plumbing implements and shoe repair materials.
There's even space for a small seat, under which is a useful supply of home brew.

Shed philosopher

It's a little hard to put your finger on exactly what it is that Jeffrey
does in his shed. He listens to the radio, smokes his pipe, has
a home-brew beer occasionally (a good drop, too) and, in his own words,
"renovates cardboard boxes." In short, he revels in his shed,
pondering its qualities and generally considering life.
That's fine, Jeffrey. That's what sheds are for.

The male end

Graham and his family live out in the bush in a sort of semicircle of buildings that were once "temporary" but have now become permanent. On the far tip of one side of this semicircle is Graham's shed.

Towards the middle of the semicircle are the kids' rooms and the kitchen and family area. On the far side of the arc is his partner Vicki's sewing workroom, full of doilies, lace, dresses and Victorian ladies' gewgaws. It's a spectrum which embraces both a masculine and feminine sense of order, and is a clever solution to the usual problem of the "ownership" of domestic space.

And there's nothing significant about the swastika stencilled on the dressmaker's dummy.

The best home workshop in the state, without a doubt

Geoff's a Ford man. He has dozens of car manuals and a vast tool collection
for working on his beloved Fords. A successful retired garage proprietor,
he spends long hours in his workshop, fine-tuning his panel van
to enable it to reach very high speeds.

Not only does his shed have a specially strengthened floor, there's a luxury
for the home workshop: a hoist. It's a pretty neat shed, too. Geoff says
he signed a contract with his wife to keep it clean.

Geoff's shed has a claim to fame: it was officially opened by Joh Bjelke-
Petersen, the then Premier of Queensland, in a shed-launching party.
There's even a small plaque, unveiled at the time, proclaiming this fact.

When you get married,
buy a shed

These two men have lived across the road from each other since childhood and have been hanging out in Graeme's shed (that's Graeme on the right and Steve on the left) ever since.

His shed, Graeme says, is "nothing special", but it has all the basics required for a classic shed: the beer fridge covered in stickers, framed posters of FJ Holdens, a fine collection of blues CDs and tapes, a mighty solid workbench (fished out of a nearby river), a potbelly stove to make it habitable during the winter, and even — a rarity these days — a calendar featuring a topless woman.

Graeme is slowly fixing up a 1948 BSA Bantam. His advice for young blokes when they get married is "buy a shed — you need a space to call your own."

The tragedy of the shedless

Eric lives in a rented house, and he's a shed orphan. Landlords take a dim view of tenants setting up sheds. They probably worry that one day they may have to clean them up.

Lamenting the plight of the tenant, Eric says, "A rented shed is never quite yours. You can't get settled down." Layers of personal history are not allowed to accumulate in a rented shed. There's no chance of developing a rich stew of objects and projects, safe in the knowledge that they can rest undisturbed for years on end if necessary.

What does this un-met yearning do for the shedless? They hang around the sheds of others or just shut that part of their lives off completely. The flat dweller, the urbanly consolidated, the tenant, have all had to anaesthetise the urge to have a good shed. There's probably a whole new range of therapy opportunities opening up . . .

The social shed

It would be a mistake to assume that the suburbs of Australia are populated with glum men sitting idly in their sheds tinkering with tools and bits of wood.

There are plenty of sheds out there that are virtually the centre of family life. For instance, it is the tradition in some Australian-Mediterranean families that many of the messier jobs of family life take place not in the main house but in the shed. The killing of livestock clearly cannot happen in the sparklingly clean kitchen. The same goes for cooking large meals for family events — it's better to let the smell stink out the shed

rather than have it permeate the house. Canning and preserving the products of the home garden is another example. Likewise, the making and sharing of home-brew beer is now a massive shed pastime. All these activities help to reinforce family links and traditions, in addition to being good fun.

In Australian culture there is also the purpose-built party shed, an example of which, sadly, was not found for this book. The distinguishing feature of this possibly mythological shed is the bare concrete floor, which slopes down to a central drainage point. This facilitates cleaning up on the morning after the party:

a hose is brought in and all spilt beer, cigarette ash, vomit and assorted party by-products are flushed away, allowing the shed to return to more mundane purposes.

Specialised beer-cooling facilities are another feature of the party shed. These facilities could be anything from a row of partially broken-down domestic fridges or special cooling troughs. Barbecues are generally associated with such sheds, especially the massive purpose-built type that can accommodate 300 sausages and 150 chops at the same time. A row of coloured lights along the rafters can often be a sign that what appears to be a normal shed is, in fact, a closet party shed.

However, these are the exception. Social sheds can be of the most benign kind, such as the family rumpus room.

By lining the walls with plywood and improving the floor surface, a functional and reasonably clean place can be created that's ideally suited to storing teenagers for long periods of time.

Like so many of our concepts about sheds, the rumpus room derives heavily from American cultural influences of the 1950s. How many of the baby-boomer generation recall all those *Popular Mechanics* magazines, showing a genial pipe-smoking Dad in a check flannel shirt labouring away on a project while a couple of freckle-faced kids watched on in admiration? The impact of those influences is still being felt in sheds around the country as those former freckle-faced children attempt to recreate the myth of the Handy Dad.

The party shed

Dave and his wife Carole have converted his garage into
a party shed/bar known as the Trade Union Tavern. It's a pub in
their own backyard, featuring decorations from around the world.
Ned Kelly stands behind the bar, his arms folded defiantly.
Photos decorate the walls in proof of the many parties that have
taken place here. There's also a Lenin corner — John Lennon on
one side, Vladimir Illych Lenin on the other.

Party sheds take many forms.

The rumpus room

This is Simon's family rumpus room. It was once a shed but has now
been lined, carpeted and decorated with sundry Americana.
This sort of conversion was a sizeable building job, yet it didn't require
the local council's permission, nor a degree in engineering.
It's a perfect demonstration of domestic male capability.

Rumpus rooms were the sorts of things you read about in *Popular Mechanics*
magazines in the 1950s and '60s. A slightly more legitimate sort of space
than your classic shed, the rumpus room still offers the opportunity for
the sort of experimentation and exploration not possible in the main house.

Simon is pleased with the fact that the kids can muck around here safely
and that parties can be held without too much concern for cleanliness.
He would possibly allow limited indoor footy in this rumpus room.

Inner-city farmhouse

Francesco's shed is a kind of farmhouse, even though he lives in an
inner-city suburb. It's here he keeps the tools for his highly productive
garden, preserves and makes sauces from vegetables, and stores
the chook food. There's also a stove that may prove useful for cooking up
big meals which would otherwise fill the main house — proudly scrubbed
clean and bright as a button — with smells.

The shed is the place where, back in the old country, the significant
seasonal events took place. For this reason it's an important part of
the family's cultural life.

Backyard bakers

Ross's shed is part of another intensively cultivated inner-suburban backyard. The main focus is the traditional domed Calabrian oven, which produces crusty wood-oven bread.

Every Saturday morning before dawn, Ross and his brothers go down to their father's backyard and fire up the oven, burning packing-crate timber and eucalypt wood to heat the brick. Meanwhile they mix the flour, water and yeast in another shed. As the dough rises they check the temperature of the oven by cooking slivers of dough and testing its internal consistency. When the tub of dough has risen and the oven is judged close to ready, they slice the dough with the casual efficiency of a job learned by time and tradition. The oven is swept clean of ash, the loaves slid in on long-handled wooden shovels and the door closed.

As the bread bakes, its massive rich smell billows over the neighbours' yards. Finally, Ross and his brothers sample some home-grown wine and enjoy homemade salami and marinated fennel accompanied by fresh hot bread dipped in olive oil . . .

Shedoscope

For many years, John had a 15-seat cinema in his shed.
Back in the early 1960s it was relatively cheap and easy to get
8 mm sound feature versions of recently released films. So John's
friends and neighbours would gather on a Saturday night to watch the
latest John Wayne epic or Gidget movie. There were curtains on the walls,
dimable lights, a bio box — in fact, the full cinematic experience in
the back shed. Unfortunately, the rise and rise of the video has meant
that the back-shed movie theatre is no longer viable, and John's
cinema has fallen into disuse.

A shed gives you hope

Geoff's shed is, in his own words, a world of its own.
A former Telecom employee, Geoff is an expert at restoring old phones,
especially those from the earlier part of this century. His shed is a busy spot
because it is very much a social centre for other old telephone specialists
who gather to barter, swap and generally natter about old phones and parts.
With a potbelly stove for winter warmth, the dog for company and, of course,
a telephone, it's a fairly sophisticated and comfortable shed.

Geoff clearly derives great benefit from his hideaway. "You can't get out
of physiotherapy what you get out of your shed," he says.

Bert's boxing shed

Bert and his boxing shed are an institution in his neighbourhood.
They've both been there for about 30 years. Bert built the shed
in his backyard not long after he came out from Ireland. Even now
his accent is so thick that one has to listen carefully to his tales of
promising youngsters who have come and gone, some gone on
to better things, some gone bad.

After nearly 20 years he still works as a bouncer in the local pub.
With surprising speed and force he can give a quick demo of how to
turn around a troublesome customer. He's still a hard man.

Skipping or doing speedball work among deformed punching
bags, the local youngsters pay close attention to his instructions.
This is a serious shed. No fooling around here.

The garage band

No collection of shed photos would be complete without the obligatory garage band. "Garage band" has become synonymous with harsh and noisy music — which is how most music tends to sound in an empty tin shed.

Here are Cane and his mates, thrashing out their own versions of rock/grunge/funk in Mum's garage. It's a place of noise and fun, of youthful dreaming of fame and fortune. The neighbours hate it.

Dedicated garage band enthusiasts get serious and start collecting old mattresses, egg cartons and ancient curtains in order to line the walls to produce that perfect, low-budget acoustic environment. Once that happens, they'll never be out of there.

The shed economy

Thousands of Australian businesses have started in the back shed. From humble origins, massive businesses have grown into vast factories and corporate empires spanning the globe.

On the other hand, thousands of businesses have also been quite happy to stay in the shed, tinkering around and making enough to get by. These are our true shed heroes: decent people who aren't out to make the big quid but will generally do a pretty good job at a fair price.

Without a massive corporate infrastructure to support, such people can ease themselves out of business towards the end of their working lives while still dabbling as the whim takes them. None of that shock-of-retirement nonsense for them.

It's also possible for them to conduct their business at a leisurely pace. If a mate drops around, you can generally find the time to share a beer or a cup of coffee. You can always come back later to finish the job you left off.

A sense of capability is very important to many of these shed owners. Having the ability to make something useful, valued, well made and functional is a boost to the shed owner's self-esteem.

Many retired captains of industry (especially engineers) have fantastic sheds. They have the resources and the skills to get together sheds that are the equivalent of small factories. Lathes, pipe benders, drill presses, saws and dozens of other pieces of large machinery can be found in many of these well-equipped sheds. Their owners are often secretive about what they contain, partly because the contents are so valuable.

What is also surprising is how many of these shed owners know of the existence of each other's sheds. There's a whole network of specialist shed people out there: during the writing of this book, many shed owners recognised each other or suggested the names of others who had sheds worth looking at. "Ted's your man to see about old lawn-mower parts," or, "If it's bending glass you want, speak to Kevin. Here's his number."

Even more interesting is the semi-cashless nature of this hidden sector of the economy. Beer currency is common (that is, one slab for a bit of welding), or just a notional exchange of built-up favours that can be called upon at some future date when they may be necessary.

For the sake of avoiding undesirable scrutiny from the taxation authorities it may be better to say no more . . .

The serious backyard workshop

George's shed is more of a small backyard factory than a shed.
A retired engineer, George has bought up old government machinery
whenever it's become obsolescent, or the contents of old workshops when
they've closed down. Consequently he has at his disposal the same capability
to bend, shape and cut metal as a small metalworking factory.

It's a large shed that has grown from a two-car garage to a space
three times that size, encompassing and enclosing a tree and having
distinct sections for different activities.

There's a sense of relentless activity about the place; such massive and
ordered productivity must have required a great deal of energy and drive.
Any large Australian city would have hundreds of people like George
labouring away in their backyard workshops.

In case you were wondering, that's an Ariel Square 4 in the foreground.

Just about anything

Rob is a resourceful man. Here, in the smaller of his two sheds,
he restores motorbikes, makes moulds, casts metal parts and even makes
his own nuts and bolts. A wide range of metalworking machinery gives his little
home workshop the capacity to make authentic parts for motorcycles and model
steam trains. The quality and detail of the finished job is extraordinary:
tiny oil pumps, secured by minute handmade bolts, pump oil through
copper pipes half the thickness of a matchstick. Rob is basically self-taught —
he just likes making things at home.

While he can cast a wide range of hard-to-get motorcycle and car parts,
he doesn't want to turn it into a production line. "It's just a hobby," says Rob.
"I mainly make things for mates."

"I wouldn't pay anybody to do anything I can do myself"

Bob is a busy man (a government minister at the time of this photograph) and values the break from work that his garage-cum-shed affords him. As a former metalworker he's very proud of his manual skills. "I wouldn't pay anybody to do anything I can do myself," he says, displaying some of the tools he has made in the past.

Bob's workshop is not the standard corrugated iron shed but the understorey of his home. This is a common form of shed in some parts of Australia.

81

Fertility and hard work

Napoleon's shed is too small and dark inside to photograph.
It contains gardening tools and rows of preserves, olives and olive oil.
Made from flattened oil drums and second-hand corrugated iron and
featuring large, overhanging eaves that create a shaded outside work space,
the shed is an important part of Napoleon's small and highly productive
backyard farm. Many years diligent work have turned the poor soil of
his family's original building block into a fertile little market garden.

Instruments for creation

David's main source of income is to sell old tools through a market stall. Sheds are the places where his potential stock lies, elusive antique tools perhaps 200 years old waiting to be discovered. "They're instruments for creation," says David, "and they usually come with interesting people full of great stories to tell. My stall attracts these sort of blokes. It's a sort of exchange point for memories."

David uses his own shed as a place to clean up old tools before their sale. The trick is to remove as much of the rust and gunge as possible but to make sure that both the metal and wood have the patina that comes from years of use and contact with the hand.

85

The shed professional

Les works for a shed manufacturer that goes by the reassuring name of "Galeprufe". As such, he's in an excellent position to tell us in which direction the Australian shed is going. Les says that as steel is now cheaper than timber, most sheds today are all steel construction instead of part timber, part steel. Sheds are, on average, also getting bigger, with a greater demand for sheds up to 30' x 20' x 8'.

According to Les, the shed is increasingly being seen as part of the family's living arrangements. Due to ever-tighter planning restrictions there is a growth in heritage sheds — the mock neo-federation shed, complete with finials and similar decorations designed to blend in with the neighbourhood. Shed purists may consider such attempts to disguise the classic galvanised simplicity of the shed a travesty and an insult.

Fathers and sons (and daughters too)

Is there a secret knowledge that men hand on to their sons in sheds? What values are handed on by older men to young men in the seclusion of the shed? Is there a case for saying that the shed is the equivalent of the Navajo smokehouse or the Papuan Longhaus, to which only men are admitted?

Surely there's a massive amount of anthropological work yet to be done on this curly subject. Then again, maybe it's better left alone; we blokes don't want that sort of interference.

During the compilation of this book, a number of men

pointed out that if you wanted to have some sort of chat with your father, you had to go out to the shed. Conversation tends to be a by-product of the endeavour at hand, be it straightening nails extracted from old timber or holding onto something while Dad works on it. Working on cars is a classic example of an occasion where things are learnt by experience and observation. Once it was almost considered automatic that sons learnt "handy" skills from their fathers in this way. Nowadays there are different kinds of domestics spaces (flats and smaller houses) and infinitely more glamorous rivals for the attentions of young men: television, video games and different social options. The shed simply cannot compete.

Most blokes need a reason or an excuse to enjoy one another's company. It's not a comfortable subject for them to discuss. Many men seemed a little hesitant to talk about the pleasure of spending time with their fathers or sons, unless they were reminiscing about the past.

Perhaps the secret message that has to be said nowadays is, "Look son, it's all right to be handy about the house, there's no shame in it. You can work on being sensitive at some other time . . ."

The early-matured shed

Paul is reasonably proud of his shed because, while it's not all that old, it has managed to acquire an air of being a mature site of worthy accumulated stuff — like good cheese. Notice, for instance, the large collection of timber offcuts beside Paul's head. This is a man who has clearly embraced the shed principle that you should never throw anything out if you think it might be useful.

His son Rogan spends some time in the shed with him, but it's hard to tell whether any secret father-to-son knowledge has passed between them.

Paul has 11 ladders. He didn't say anything about it; a friend of his, easily impressed by such information, came up with this fact. Modesty concerning one's shed is definitely a good thing.

Learning by osmosis

Three generations (from left: Matthew, Allan and John) are shown here
sharing a shed. "I can make a mess in the shed and it's all right because
I make the rules," says Allan. It's been a highly productive mess over the years,
with cupboards, chairs, a boat and bassinets all finding their way here.
John observes that whatever he learnt about woodworking and repairing
he gained by osmosis rather than through direct instruction.
This is very much the preferred way for generations to hand on
secret male-to-male knowledge.

A dream that one day . . .

Terry says that sheds are a space to dream in — a place of limitless possibilities waiting to happen. Even though his own shed tends to get used for drying washing and as a sorting area, he still intends to get around to make something of it. "You see a lot of half-finished projects in sheds," says Terry.

And yes, that's a Stanley knife that his son is proudly holding in his hand.

Dick's daughters

Dick's shed is a place of memory. At his funeral, one of his daughters sprinkled over his coffin shavings gathered from the floor of his shed instead of the traditional rose petals. Now, more than a year after his death, the shed provides a link to his memory for his daughters and sons-in-law. Talking of her father, one daughter draws in the air the outline of the old man standing at his bench, invoking a startlingly imaginable figure. Another picks up an odd little cup made from a cut-down jam tin and muses over its practical economy. Dick was a man far ahead of his time in recycling and other sound environmental habits.

It's a wonderful shed. A lifetime's collection of skills and knowledge have been condensed into a practical order that is at once systematic yet agreeably casual: tools clustered together on a rack made with a few artful twists of wire; latches, handles and hinges made from carefully cut and soldered metal and wire. There's no waste here.

For the family, the shed poses a quandary: what should happen to this space? Should it be preserved as a common family area (great for the sons-in-law to come down and use the power tools), or will its contents start to rust from lack of care and attention now that the shed's busy days are over? The answer seems clear. The pull of the shed is strong, and having survived this long, it will probably see a few more serviceable years yet.

Retiring to the bench

Australian men retire to their sheds and then they die. This elephant's graveyard view of the Australian shed should be tempered with another view: without a shed to go to, Australian men would probably die even more quickly.

Many retired men feel that their shed is a lifeline. Behind the sniggers and the jokes from some quarters it is obvious that there is a genuine need for men to have a meditative space that allows for both creative expression and purposeful activity.

In the sheds of retired men around Australia there is also an extraordinary amount of accumulated skill and talent not being put to use. Such is the distrust and uncertainty between the generations, however, that there is unlikely to be a spontaneous outbreak of cranky old metalworkers giving wayward youths useful tips on fixing up their clapped-out Holdens or demonstrating the glory of the ancient art of brazing.

A number of the older shed owners interviewed during the research for this book *did* mention that they would quite like to pass on their skills, but mostly they were too shy to do so. This is a sorry situation, but perhaps sorrier still is the state of shedlessness which afflicts many elderly men. Shedlessness is most evident when older couples move into a retirement village: a rich shed, an accumulation of up to 60 years of shed activity, must be culled down to a few small handtools or, worse still, nothing at all. Those retirement homes that don't allow men a little space to muck around in are especially tragic. Space is already at a premium in such places. No wonder some of their inhabitants often feel that a useful life is over.

Retirement can be a stressful business. Some men positively look forward to the shed in their retirement; they view it as a focus for creative activities denied them in their working lives. One man spoke of a neighbour, a former police officer, who the day after his retirement went out and bought a substantial wood lathe because he'd always dreamed of the unique satisfaction of revealing the beauty of timber on a humming lathe.

For some men, retirement brings a realisation that despite a lengthy working life as a breadwinner, they have few friends and that the friends they had at work were only acquaintances with whom they shared the hours 9 'til 5. Some men contrast the way in which women seem to establish better friendships with other women. These are troubling matters for all men to consider, but perhaps particularly so for the retired man.

Ted

This is a shed which has truly seen a lifetime of experience. Ted, its owner, a former electrician at Holden's, retired some time in the 1950s. Since then he has put his shed to good use. It has a comprehensive range of equipment for the home workshop, with plenty of well-made storage drawers (those old Singer treadle sewing machine drawers have found many a happy home in a shed).

On the bench is a small homemade steam engine in the process of being soldered together from old cans and pipes as a gift for a distant great-grandchild. Toys that demonstrated the basic principles of physics such as this were once quite common but have since been replaced by SegaMegadrives and suchlike. It's nice to know that someone's still making the stuff that makes you think.

Busier than ever

Down the end of this shed, creepers have started to strangle some old kids' bicycles. But in the middle, newly varnished croquet mallets hang from the roof. Even though he's retired, ex-woodwork teacher Alan still passes on his valuable skills. Several times a week he teaches young women the basics of woodworking. He shows off their work with an offhand dismissiveness that does not conceal a certain pride in their achievements under his tutelage.

Like so many men who find that their skills are still sought even in retirement, Alan wonders how he ever had time to work. Nevertheless, he appreciates the fact that now he can choose to do things when he feels like it.

A local institution

Josef has retired with his wife to a small seaside town, where he has
established a substantial shed in the backyard. It's very important to him.
"I'd be lost without it," he says. "You might as well put me in
a pine box as separate me from my shed."

Although Josef's shed is connected to the main house by an intercom,
it has many useful domestic features, including various cooking arrangements
(great for barbecuing local seafood) and an enormous cool room
with a very substantial supply of home-brew beer.

Clearly, Josef has a well-set-up shed. The locals speak of it with admiration.

A place to relax

Joe has a compact shed in which he enjoys a daily afternoon nap.
It's a very organised little space with all manner of tools tucked away
behind curtains. There's even an old treadle sewing machine ideal for
stitching canvas, a by-product of spending some of his life working as a rigger.
Joe is well known in his neighbourhood as a handy person when
it comes to repairing things made of canvas and rope.

Don's multi-function workshop

Don is a retired cabinet maker. His shed, which is in fact a series of
rooms dedicated to various hobbies such as wood turning and gem cutting,
is a well-ordered space. This is often the case with retired craftsmen,
who regard an orderly work space as a matter of professional pride.
Don still makes beautifully finished wooden objects, such as the fishing
floats by his right hand. His tools are kept in immaculate condition.

There's another reason why Don's shed is important to him:
his young family lived in it while the main house was being built.
It then became a billiards room for his family as they grew up.
Now it's a workshop for Don in his retirement.

Solutions for retirement villages

Retirement homes present quite a problem for some men. The act of moving from a normal suburban house with space for a shed is fraught with problems: frequently the shed and its contents are disposed of in order to fit into a small unit. Retirement homes have been slow to recognise the sense of loss that some men experience when this happens. However, Herb and Dean (left and right) and some of their retirement village friends have avoided this problem by using a double garage as a workshop for their shared use. It has become a major focus of activity and is even seen by the village owners as a marketing advantage.

Herb, Dean and their friends share tools (a delicate matter) and skills, and it's an enjoyable form of socialising for them. "We don't have to worry about time in here," says Herb.

The men joke about how their shed is a bit of a glorified kennel.

The illicit shed

Some sheds never made it to this book. This is because their owners were conscious that their shed activities were not likely to bring approval from various authorities, be they the police or the politically correct.

Top of the list are the home-brewed firewater makers. It seems that nearly every culture has a tradition of making grappa, slivovitz, shed vodka, scrumpy, cherry wine, whatever — as long as it's as near to pure alcohol as possible. Aware of the illegality of their activities, Australian distillers of these fiery liquors go to extraordinary lengths to conceal their distilling apparatus and the operations of their sheds.

One elderly gentleman, who had spent some time in a POW camp after the war, had mastered the art of quickly disassembling his still and scattering its components around the shed so as to seem part of the general shed paraphernalia.

Growing marijuana under lights is another highly illicit shed activity. This involves large quantities of electricity, complex switches and watering systems and a very high level of paranoia. One shed dope grower even had an extraction fan with an extremely high chimney to diffuse the resinous smell of his activities.

Pornography and sheds seem to be strongly connected in many people's minds. A number of those interviewed could recall going to someone's shed at some time in their youth for a buck's night and watching blue movies. Videos may have killed this tradition. The shed with pin-ups of nude women seemed fairly uncommon.

Another type of shed that was not willing to be exposed was the war gamer's shed. At least one militaria fan has a shed filled with full-size trenches, barbed wire, dried mud and duckboards. The idea is to get dressed up in First World War uniforms, grab some beers and sit in a dugout for the afternoon with your mates, listening to 78s on a wind-up record player and getting drunk. The players involved in these activities didn't want to be photographed, as they said people wouldn't understand.

Men like the illegitimacy of the shed. It's not quite acceptable; a shed is for outcasts. If there's anything that's been pinched or is a bit dodgy, it's probably in the shed.

Handy tips for the would-be shed owner

Good basic tools

With the growth in recent years of do-it-yourself culture, many people have gone out and bought themselves tools, often without any understanding of what they should be looking for or what they should be avoiding.

It's unfortunate that there are a great number of very poor quality handtools on the market. As a general rule, cheap tools are to be avoided; they are usually made from poor quality metal and are of such shoddy construction that they will prove your apparently modest investment to be a complete waste of money. There are still good quality tools for sale, generally in specialised hardware and tool shops. They're often expensive, but if looked after will provide many years of good service.

Another option is to buy tools at garage sales, where many a tradesman's tools have gone for a song. It's also true that there are collectors and dealers out there who know exactly how much such tools are worth, so be forewarned.

What to look for

Planes

The bases of most planes aren't 100 per cent level, so it's useful to take a good engineer's rule or steel straightedge with you when you're looking for a second-hand plane.

To check that a plane is not warped or bowed, retract the blade or cutter and lay the straightedge along the base of the plane. There should only be a hair's width of light showing between the plane and the straightedge.

The plane should be clean and in good condition. The cutter is most important; check to see that the back of the blade is not pitted with rust. If it is, it will be impossible to get a sharp edge across the complete width of the blade. Brands and makes to look out for include early Stanley, Record, and the red and black Pope Falcon. Most older American-made planes are pretty good. Steer clear of Chinese-made or Carter planes.

Chisels

Quality brands of chisels to look out for include E.A. Berg (with a blue shark on the handle), Ward, Stanley, Titan and older Marples. There are also a number of very good Swiss brands of chisels. Again, it's important to check that the back is not pitted, otherwise it will be difficult to make a sharp edge.

Saws

Don't buy a bent or kinked saw. It's almost impossible to straighten and will be practically useless. Old saws can be sharpened by a professional saw sharpener (look in the phone book for one near you), bringing impressive improvements for only about $8 to $10.

Good older brands include Philadelphia Diston, Spear and Jackson, Pax, Simonds, Sandersons and Sandvik. As a rough rule of thumb, if it has five holding screws in the handle and is marked London Spring on the blade, it should be very good.

Again, saws of more recent manufacture, even from some of the reputable brands mentioned above, are not necessarily good, so take care in choosing a new saw.

Hammers

A good claw hammer is a must. Don't buy one that has a chipped face — it could deflect dangerously.

The feel of a hammer is probably the most important thing to take into consideration when buying one, as there are not many working parts to go wrong. Bear in mind that a hammer shouldn't be too heavy or too light for the task you have in mind. In theory, the handle of a balanced hammer resting on its claw should be absolutely horizontal. Good brands of hammers include Cheney, Stanley and Cyclone.

Squares

The best way to check whether a square is still right-angled is to place it on a solid surface with a straight edge (such as a piece of chipboard), rule a line along the edge, turn it over and rule another just parallel to it. If the two lines are not parallel, the rule is not absolutely 90 degrees. Whether purchasing a new or old square, be very wary of instruments with wooden handles, as they can warp or twist. Good brands to look out for include Rabone, Starrett and Moore & Wright.

Cleaning and looking after old tools

If you're a vigilant searcher you'll often find very good old tools, despite being covered in rust or grease. There are a number of ways of cleaning such tools. One technique is to soak them in molasses for a period of between two days and two weeks. This should remove most

rust. However, all wooden and die-cast parts should be removed from the tool before being soaked in molasses. Molasses is available from stock and feed suppliers.

It is best to experiment with this technique on something that's not of value before trying it on your tool. Some people prefer cleaning with steel-wool and methylated spirits.

Once your tool has been cleaned of rust, paint and other impurities, metal parts should be coated in CRC Longlife or a similar product.

Unless you're using the tool frequently, don't hang it up on the traditional workshop shadow board: it will end up rusting again. Instead, put it away in a dry place such as a drawer or a toolbox, preferably with a film of CRC Longlife over the tool.

If you are interested in information about or identification of older and unusual tools contact:

The Handtool Preservation Association of Australia
PO Box 1163
Carlton Victoria 3053
or

T.J. Rowe
PO Box 49
Myponga South Australia 5202.

Storage

If one is going to accumulate stuff then a bit of storage space may be needed, although just how to store things is the subject of debate among shed owners. Some people prefer random storage, which involves leaving things

where they were last put down. The pile theorists (as they're called) say this is good exercise for the brain, as it improves the memory. On the other hand there are those people who prefer to bring a little more organisation to their sheds. They like to store things on shelves and in cupboards.

Whichever system you prefer, you're probably going to need some sort of shelving. You can go down to the local hardware and buy the basic bolt-together zinc-plated steel shelving, but it's a bit uninteresting — and, some would say, overpriced. An alternative is to approach your local fruit and veg shop and ask them if they've got any old wooden boxes they don't need. Stacked one on top of another, these boxes can usually reach a respectable height before they topple over. Some of them still have nice pictures of fruit on the side.

The other option is to go to a house demolition sale. These are usually advertised in the building materials section of the classified ads. If you turn up at the right time you can often pick up some very cheap shelving and adapt it to your purposes. Many of the building demolition yards (found in the Yellow Pages under Building Materials — Second-hand) have good industrial shelving going cheap.

Shed furniture

Never ever buy a new piece of furniture for the shed. A good shed chair is one that would have been thrown out if you hadn't interceded and saved it, even if it's not quite as flash as it once was. It should be strong enough to stand on, so it may need a few extra cross braces — and while you're at it, put an extra cushion on it for comfort.

A dartboard is a vital piece of shed furniture. So too is a picture of Queen Elizabeth II. It doesn't need to indicate any royalist tendencies; rather, it's a sign that the shed is a reservoir of memories and old associations.

Most essential of all is a stable, solid workbench. It needs to be strong enough to withstand something being belted onto its surface with a large hammer. A good test of stability is to jump up and down on top of it; if the bench doesn't move, it's acceptable. Some people prefer traditional wooden workbenches, but the welded steel variety is just as good and likely to be cheaper. Secondhand workbenches are found at garage sales, in junkyards or at auctions.

Now you've got a bench, you'll need a vice to go on it as well. Metal vices are all the go these days — wood vices are relatively rare and are more expensive.

The beer fridge

Sheds get hot in summer, so a beer fridge is a must. The best kind is the large, rounded type, preferably with a lot of chrome. It's often a bit noisy, but at least this tells you the electricity's still on. You might have to keep the door shut with an octopus strap. Then put lots of stickers on it.

Shed radio

The shed radio is one that has been superseded in the house by the all-new CD-playing AM/FM black plastic box.

Inevitably, the shed radio is AM only, and thus is only good for listening to the races or the ranting and raving of talkback pocket-despots.

There are even those serious radio listeners who have had a phone installed in the shed in order to respond to some outrage on the air ("I was just so furious when I heard that young fellow that I had to ring up to say . . .").

Ideally, a good shed radio should have a warm, fuzzy tone, with the speaker hidden behind some of that strange flecked cloth that only ever appeared on 1940s and '50s radios and on your old aunt's large scratchy furniture.

The radio should be of durable construction — something able to withstand a lump of timber powerfully directed towards it — and be missing at least one vital knob. If it has to be switched on and off with a pair of pliers, so much the better.

A television is a rare thing in a shed — unless it's a shed of the totally malignant variety. This is because it's pretty difficult to do something useful and watch TV at the same time. The spirit of the Australian shed poses one of the greatest threats to the universal dominance of television over the minds of the populace.

The true music lover

The genuine connoisseur of good music does not depend on his shed radio as a source of the quality product. He brings his own.

Hence it's possible to find many a shed with a fine collection of greasy but dearly loved tapes ("I always listen to Elmore James when I'm working on a gearbox"). Country and western and blues both fall into the category of favoured shed music, possibly because both are often a little too gritty or maudlin — or worse still, old fashioned — for main-house domestic tastes.

The true shed fan, of course, listens to his music on an 8-track cartridge player. This has the unfortunate problem of restricting the listening range to the three or so years at the end of the 1960s — a period heavily dominated by Perry Como. This shortcoming is, however, compensated for by the pleasure of wiring up a car audio system out of its native environment.

Where do you get a shed from anyway?

This is the easy part. Sheds are big business, and the competition to sell you a shed is cutthroat.

A distinction needs to be drawn between tool sheds and garages. A tool shed is generally a small, flimsy production designed to hold gardening tools and to be less than the minimum size required for council approval.

A garage, on the other hand, is big enough to more than swing a cat, especially if you don't put the car in it. A garage is an ideal basis for a shed.

Shop around for a shed that suits your needs. You can buy garages or tool sheds in kit form or even get them built by tradesmen on your behalf. However, keeping in the spirit of the thing, it's more interesting to explore wider possibilities.

Second-hand sheds

Many older garages are simply made from steel and timber frames bolted together and covered in galvanised iron. It's possible to buy a garage of this kind very cheaply at a demolition sale. All you have to do is pour a slab of cement for the floor, dismantle the structure and reassemble it in your own backyard. That way your new shed will be well on the way to acquiring its veneer of shed credibility — even if it's someone else's.

Other built structures

The bodies of old vans, pantechnicons and other trucks make a fine basis for a shed. Again, they already have that friendly, used look about them. Never mind that they get hot as Hades in the summer.

You could always make a shed yourself from old sheets of metal and backyard junk. You may need a few essential framing pieces from the many handyman iron and steel shops that sell iron sections, purlins, frames and so forth (check farming magazines and newspapers for details on these).

You can improvise. Reuse the old iron from the garden fence if the metal is not too far gone. If you make your shed just under the minimum size for council approval, use your imagination to expand it.

With the unending gentrification of most Australian suburbs, some local councils have become design fascists, tightly regulating the appearance of local sheds to fit their notions of order and civic pride. Would you be able to get away with old hammered-out oil tins for a wall? Not if the local council hears about it. It's always best to make a few tentative inquiries first. If you're planning an extensive range of enjoyable activities in your shed, it's advisable to keep your drawings to a bare minimum. Councils get a little concerned when they see lined walls, extensive power points and so on.

STORIES FROM
THE SHED

Introduction

Wood Block

PEOPLE ARE KEEN to talk about sheds. It strikes a nerve deep down. It's something to do with men, Australian men, and it runs across all classes, all ethnic backgrounds, the city and the country.

Stories from the Shed is a successor to the book *Blokes and Sheds*, which talked around the issues mentioned above. It comes about partly as a result of many letters received both before and after the publication of that book.

Readers may find some of the contributions are overwhelmingly nostalgic and sentimental. Yet there is more to this than the simple invoking of some golden era in Australia's past. No-one is saying we should actually go back to the good old days; but there seems to be a need for saying where we come from, as a means of placing modern life in some sort of context.

Perhaps it's just the need to reattach oneself to some kind of certainty. Sheds seem to be part of a collective memory and a trigger for finding a personal history that allows people to make sense of the past and deal with the future. There are many thousands of those little personal museums out there.

But it's not as simple as that either. To the politically correct, there's the strong whiff of male backlash against feminism about shed culture; some people feel that there's something wrong or weird here that needs a firm hand to get in there and *correct it*.

Backlash is too strong a word; if there is a backlash it's an uncertain and contradictory one for the most part. Most men would agree if pushed that the impact of feminism has resulted in many positive changes. Yet there's a simmering resentment about having been pigeonholed as the bad guy, the guilty party. Many men feel that nothing they can do or say is going to meet the approval of the morally superior and "them" in charge.

Meanwhile, the authority that was once handed to men as a birthright has been diluted and diffused. There's not so much certainty about the role of men any more. Not that there were ever any easy guidebooks on how to be a man; paradoxes abound. There are still many expectations that men should be at least partly the tough guy, partly the sensitive spiritual type. A bit of Clint Eastwood mixed in with a touch of the Dalai Lama.

It's a bit of a tall order.

The shed becomes the place where you call off the bluff. You're just you. There are no Joneses to keep up with in the shed. Appearances are not kept up. The mask drops.

Even if life feels empty, the shed is not hollow — it can be richly packed, dense with things and stuff. It is materialistic without being consumerist. It can be an opportunity for a full-on assault of all senses: big stinks, loud noises, bad language, complete chaos and disorder.

There's a more subtle appeal to the senses, too. To run the hands along freshly sanded timber, stripped back to reveal hidden form and beauty. And then the varnish to give brilliant depth. Such beauty can be deeply and silently appreciated. There is no need for words.

Some sheds are like a good piece of blues — soulful and dark, speaking about pain and loss, the contemplation of the failure of life's expectations, failure generally. Gritty, dirty, decaying and furtive. But these qualities are not all negative: because like the blues, there can be the germ of repair and healing within. There is depth and substance.

Isolation is a recurring theme in sheds. This, too, is paradoxical. There are benefits from such isolation; contemplation and meditation in a calm place away from the hurly-burly of the world. A surprising number of men talk about sheds using words and images that show a strongly spiritual and religious aspect of shed ownership.

On the other hand sheds can be shells that men hide in, away from others, when they could benefit from contact with people. Michael Lee's closing article draws on his working experiences to point out some tragic outcomes of such isolation.

There are lots of stories about fathers in this collection. By far the majority of stories received dealt with the contributor's father or grandfather. Most of these contributors were women. Writers of both sexes strongly identify their fathers with the shed.

Some of the stories are about the re-evaluation of fathers. They may have seemed distant and inarticulate, some even a touch tyrannical, but the passage of time has softened the memory and the more painful edges have been knocked off. To be taciturn and blunt was a sign of strength; verbal diarrhoea and the expression of emotion was weakness. In retrospect some of those men acted the way they understood to be the best. In their sheds they found the strength to get through life.

Mark Thomson

The Corrugated Kingdom

Many worshippers of the tin temple feel very possessive about their tiny corrugated kingdom. The shed is a sort of personal republic, where the occupant can be *el Presidente*, Minister for Everything, the benevolent dictator, you name it. Some of these stories serve as an introduction to the current state of play in the world of sheds.

Alice in Shedland

WHEN WE MOVED to a caravan, Ray insisted he had to have a shed. How could I, a female and a foreigner, understand?

He tried to buy a second-hand shed. People leaving town often had them for sale but they were far too big.

"A 10 by 10 footer," he sighed. "That's all I want." No metrics in shedland. "Remember my shed in Adelaide?"

Did I remember? He went west to work on the mines, leaving me to pack everything for a trans-continental move. After several cartons of tools and garden implements I gave up in despair. A "genuine Aussie battler" hired from the want ads of a local newspaper got what was left — and was paid $30 for his trouble.

"You what? You did what?" Shock and disbelief crackled down the STD line. Gone forever were a dozen cans of paint with a tablespoonful in each. A bottle of kero. A bottle of turps. Some wood. A lounge chair with the stuffing falling out. Pin-up girls. Bits of metal. Cable ties. Flowerpots. Half a bag of cement.

'You sold my shelves? That was heavy-duty pallet racking. For how much?" His moan echoed through the long-distance ether.

The caravan and annex required constant fine-tuning. All of it would have been easier if he had had his cans of old bolts, screws, washers and nuts. He never nagged, just left tools and tape measures on the coffee table and bookcase. Jars of screws and bolts mixed uneasily in the kitchen cupboard with spices and herbs. He was right, he had to have a shed. Phone calls were made. The Visa card was accepted. A shed was on the way.

A few days later a box appeared on the lawn. What sort of shed was this? All he got for his money was a box about 10 feet tall, 1 foot wide and 10 inches deep. He tried to sound confident. No worries, the shed crew would sort it out tomorrow.

His mates arrived early in varying states of distress caused by the night before. Over coffee the merits of tek screws, pop rivets and cordless drills were discussed. Plans were examined. Stories of legendary sheds from the past were exchanged. Many pieces of metal were laid out on the lawn.

I fled.

Much later, when I returned, a gleaming silver shed stood in the corner of the yard. He was sitting nearby with a beer.

"Want to see it?"

I stepped inside, expecting pristine empty space. No. A hammock. An old recliner chair. Some bricks. Shadecloth. Glue guns. A pin-up girl. Peatmoss. An esky. Half a bucket of sharp sand. What was all this? Where had it been?

"I had it stashed here and there," he said as we walked out. Shrugging. "It's shed stuff." And he firmly locked the door.

Margaret Van Putten, Leinster, Western Australia

The guardian angel

I BELIEVE IN guardian angels. In my first shed, a guardian angel took up residence there, in a sacred place for those who appear to be lost in a chaotic world of their own. And the guardian angel followed me to all my other sheds. This story proves it.

As a youth I was tall and skinny. I read many books on body building and was keen to acquire some weight-lifting gear. But this was the Depression of the 1930s and I realised that if I wanted something, I had to make it myself. So I bought a length of 11/4 inch steel shafting and made some lead weights to convert it into a barbell.

My body-building project involved a routine of standing and lying-down exercises. Starting with the 20 lb bar, I did each exercise five times, increasing by one until I reached 20 times. I then added 5 lb to the bar and went back to five times. Being "steadfast of purpose", I reached 20 times with the bar loaded with 30 lb of lead. Unfortunately the clips that held the lead in place kept slipping, making the whole procedure a bit dangerous. I just didn't have time to design better clips or to collect more lead so, like so many projects, it all finished up in the shed. What a pity! Had I continued I would now have been able to lift a derailed goods train back on to the tracks.

But it wasn't the end of my body-building gear. Like everything that goes into the dark void of the shed, there was no foreseeable use for it. It just went into that endless realm of possibilities that may take dozens of years to reach fulfilment.

The barbell took only a bit more than 10 years to find its purpose.

It was converted into a kind of specialised crowbar with a goose neck on one end and a sharp wedge on the other. Even now, 65 years later, I still use it.

The lead weights are another story. They travelled across the country from Melbourne to Perth when we shifted some 40 years ago. I always intended to use them to make some fishing sinkers; I had moulds and have always made my own. But the lead remained in the shed for another 17 years.

It was around the time my son John and his mate Ken took up skin diving; they had the air tanks but the lead-weight belts they bought weren't up to scratch.

John's mum was out and I was at work. Perfect. They got the heavy aluminium stockpot from the kitchen and took it down to the shed. There they dug out a beaut little camping stove of mine; it had a little pumpkin-shaped fuel tank and was run on lighter fluid. It could produce a very intense heat but it was never designed to take a huge stockpot containing 30 lbs of lead. Yet it did melt the lead and they made quite a few weights.

Just as Ken was adding some more lead, he heard an ominous click and looked down to see that the reflected heat was melting the legs of the stove. He only had time to scream "OUT!" and jump clear before the fuel tank went up with a massive bang.

They say the universe started with a big bang. As the Bible says: "The earth was without form; and void, and darkness was upon the face of the deep." And then came the Big Bang, which blew the dome of the heavens and created all the things of beauty in our world.

And so it was with our shed. The Big Bang hurled the big stockpot with its 30 lbs of lead to the roof. Not even the glory of the Vatican's dome or of any temple or cathedral has ever been so richly adorned with flimsy silver lace as the dome of my shed.

All the neighbours within half a mile rushed outside; fortunately the police did not come inquiring. The boys were OK, thanks in part to the resident guardian angel that watches over all those engaged in the creative chaos of shed activities.

Funnily enough, in wet weather the shed used to leak but since the Big Bang it never has; further proof of the guardian angel theory, I suppose.

David Bensley, Koondoola, Western Australia

Gus

WHENEVER WE ARRIVED, Granddad was always down in the shed. Nana would kiss us, wet and sloppily, brushing our cheeks with the prickly hairs on her face, and say: "Gus is down in the shed."

Nana's house was a house of rooms, and every room was different. The hallway had mirrors, umbrella stands and magazine racks. When you walked down the long strip carpet, you felt the front door close behind you.

The lounge room was always dark, with the curtains drawn. There was a rich velvet smell of the floral lounge mixed with the musty old photographs on the bureau. The big wooden television set shone with hand polishing and, on the privileged occasions we were allowed to watch it, hissed with snow and ghostly figures. Under the set was a perfectly preserved specimen of a turtle with a neat spear hole my uncle had put in the shell.

The kitchen was cold and scrubbed. The stainless-steel sink was bright under the lace-curtained window. Above the stove, the tannin-smelling teapot, cosy and caddy. The Laminex table top, where the broken freshness of sliced bread did battle with old cheese and tart gherkin.

The vestibule, where we all sat with Nana, had green lino and shelves of preserves and a big kerosene fridge.

The bedroom, with the big quilt-covered bed, smelling darkly of decay, where old postcards and letters were rummaged from a camphor-wood box on the dressing table and a big jarrah chest on the floor.

The toilet was in the laundry, across the red-painted concrete floor, next to the cement troughs and the built-in copper. A ballerina with a crocheted pink dress sat on the doorstop and another, in blue, demurely covered a spare toilet roll. The green Air-wick was always open and there was a box full of torn newspaper squares which I never chose to use.

Nana would say: "Go and tell Granddad you're here."

And I would go. I still remember the way: past the tank stand and the television mast; the high grapevine where there were white and black grapes in season and we were allowed to swallow the seeds because Nana did; the little storage shed with separate bins for wheat and pollard, an old galvanised dipper in each; the parrots in their cages, one nearly a hundred years old with a long curved beak and dangerous; to a fork in the path, where the passionfruit trellis began.

Granddad's shed was on a kind of peninsular that stuck out into the big chook yard where there were at least 20 chooks, red, white and black and several nasty roosters. His shed was built like a perfect miniature weatherboard cottage with an angled corrugated-iron roof and its own guttering. There was a paned window facing the house and another that looked out onto the chook run.

I'd knock on the tongue-and-groove wooden door and Granddad would growl: "Come in."

His shed was always tidy. Every kind of woodworking tool was hanging over its painted silhouette on the pegboard, or lying neatly in its place along the back of the bench. Every chisel and saw looked sharp, ready to cut. The hammer handles were worn with gripping, and every tool for which I had no name looked mysterious and useful. The big, solid bench was clean and the heavy vice at the end clamped shut.

In front of Granddad was always a tin of Capstan ready rubbed and a book of papers. There was always a bent cigarette between his stained fingers, and smoke hanging in the light above the windows.

Granddad would say, "Hello Boy," and tell me to tell Nana he would be in soon. I never thought to ask if he ever did any work but I noticed the little pile of wood shavings under the bench was never disturbed.

In the vestibule, Nana would finally bring out her hard and sweet home-made icecream and cut big squares of it from the aluminium tray. We would bite the chunks, putting our teeth on edge, while Mum and Nana drank cups of tea and Granddad would drink the bottle of beer that Dad had brought him and tell him it made a nice change from the cooking wine.

Stephen Faulds, Cannington, Western Australia

Simultaneous intention recognition

S<small>TORE NAILS THE HASSLE-FREE WAY</small>
Lightly hammer each nail into any exposed timber in the garage, home or garden and you will soon forget all those words you used when picking up spilt nails. And every time you need a nail, who knows, there may be one in the spot where you need it. Just knock it in all the way.

— Golly Gosh, Handy-Man Hints, *The Prospecter*, December 1978

The brother is good with his hands

The current project is top-secret and patent-pending but the whole street knows about it. A few Telstra technicians know about it, too.

"Why do you want two dedicated lines in your shed?" they asked him.

"That's restricted information, at this stage," he replied, which immediately prompted them to install a tap.

The brother is working on a telecommunications device which enables the caller to determine whether an engaged number is, in fact, engaged *because that person is attempting to call the caller*.

The device will override the connection protocol and allow the two people to make contact. The brother calls it Simultaneous Intention Recognition and claims his device will revolutionise telephony.

"We will be able to afford a holiday this year," he told the dinner table last week.

"I don't know what you think you're up to in the shed," Lilly replied, sternly, "but I am sick of the strange clicks and beeps when I use the phone."

The brother stared at her, darkly.

"And another thing," she said. "The neighbours want to know why you want them to ring you at 10.37 pm every night and, when they do, you are always engaged."

"It's none of your business," he said.

"Maybe you are developing pro-active personality withdrawal symptoms," she said.

"What on earth are you talking about?" he said.

"Oh, you know the thing," she said. "Instead of sending letters to yourself, like normal lonely people, you ask people to ring you up at a specific time so that you can leave your phone off the hook. You are trying to prove to them that you have an engaged life."

"If you knew a hundredth of what you think you know," the brother said, "you'd be an extremely irritating person."

Lilly threw a bowl of pasta at him. It was too late. He had already seen it coming. He was already out of his chair, already out the back door, already across the great black divide, already inside his warm padlocked shed.

"There goes the holiday," Lilly said, to nobody in particular.

The brother likes to fix things

"We need a new toaster," Lilly said.

"It's only 12 months old," the brother said.

"And it has lived its life," Lilly said.

"I'll take it out to the shed and have a look at it," the brother said. "Maybe I can fix it."

"You bought the cheapest one you could find in the first place," Lilly said. "Things like that aren't designed to be fixed. Things like that are designed not to be bought in the first place."

"Anything that works when you buy it, works for a reason," the brother said. "If it doesn't work now, that's for another reason. Maybe I can fix it."

"Like the vacuum cleaner that has been in the shed for three years," she said. "Why don't you fix real things like the economy, or this disastrous marriage, or the reason why people get ill the instant they give up smoking?"

"One thing at a time," the brother said.

The brother is in a hurry

"Australians are better positioned than any citizens in the world to reap the benefits of downloadable software via the internet with our untimed local-call fee structure," the brother said, but added a warning. *"This will not last."*

The brother has a lot to download before timed local calls come into play. Fonts, clipart, software, software-writing software, lists, lists of lists, software manuals, hot tips, upgrades, patches, bug-fixers, cross-system enablers, system-enhancers, system-options, system-trainers, system-writers.

The brother is in deeper than he knows. He gets on top of a sliver of it and then discovers a major upgrade for a core application which requires new patches for all the software he has already downloaded.

The sound of smashing glass in the shed.

"If I am the designated wage-earner in this household," Lilly said, recently, "perhaps I am entitled to remind you that Tuesdays are the night for putting out the Big Bin and that when you crawl into bed at 4 am on Wednesday, it tires me to ask you whether or not you have performed your minimal contribution to our contract."

"Then don't," the brother said, succinctly.

"I haven't asked you this for three weeks," Lilly replied, equally succinctly. "Noticed the bin lately? It looks like the great NYC garbage strike."

"I am constructing the communication network of this household for the rest of our lives," the brother said.

"Try sucking the other one," Lilly said.

The brother addresses domestic harmony

There were flowers on the dining table, a cocktail on the bench, Christian Maucéry through the sound system.

Lilly was immediately suspicious. "You have a lover and she is pregnant," she said. "And you want to tell me all this tonight."

The brother was crestfallen.

"And it is all over with her," Lilly continued. "Your lover has agreed to have an abortion."

He stared at her.

"She has the abortion," Lilly continued, "and can't handle it because she is young and stupid. She can't talk to you because you are a part of her stupidity. She knows that I know and wants gender assistance. I like her because she reminds me of me before I met you and I fall for her need, as you did. Against all my better judgment, *I take her on*. I do your business. I handle her guilt, your incompleteness, all that shit. You go back to the shed and I make a new friend. Is that the trick?"

"Sometimes you are seriously deranged," the brother said.

"Oh, you mean that there will be no abortion," Lilly said. "And we will have a Simultaneous Intention Recognition factor operating. One child with one father and two mothers. Is that the cocktail?"

"There is no lover, Lilly," he said.

"Really?" she said.

"Really," he said.

"Damn," she said.

John Kingsmill, Adelaide, South Australia

The workshop workshop

GOODY TWO-SHOES men can be really annoying. You know the kind. Really into the latest thing, with that special kind of earnest, basically humourless sincerity. Big on telling you about their star signs. Always off to a weekend workshop, forking out a large amount of cash to sit around in a remote patch of mud somewhere and be intense.

Frankly, many of these fellows are an embarrassment to the gender.

The problem is that these characters are "getting into" sheds as quick as you can say shadowboard. The buzz is that getting in touch with your inner handiness is definitely the next big thing. Forget those weekends rechannelling your crystals in cyberspace — the workshop workshop is where it's at.

Expect the full-colour brochure shortly. One Friday night you'll roll up to an old shed in an industrial suburb where you'll be locked up the entire weekend with a bunch of misfits. It will be sort of like a Quentin Tarantino movie without the laughs. At least your family will have the pleasure of your absence for a few days.

There'll probably be a "team leader" (inevitably a grizzled American con artist/hippy called Darrien) or perhaps a "facilitator" who's a defrocked Irish priest named Dermot or Declan.

There'll be workshop after workshop — all unplugged, of course. No point in taking any risks. Instead of whiteboards and butcher's paper there'll be diagrams drawn in sawdust on the floor. Blindfolded, you'll assemble a brace and bit and drill a hole in a piece of chipboard to the cheers and bellows of your fellow shed brothers.

There will be ample opportunity to get into the usual workshop activities. Your group (i.e. the loudest person) will obsessively analyse every little shed activity, make all-encompassing moral judgements and do a bit of simplistic pigeonholing. This then provides the ground rules for the fun bit — the persecution of the incorrect and the search for the guilty. You can be guaranteed there'll be lots of crying.

In exchange for your $2000, at the end of the weekend you'll receive an angle grinder autographed by Kevin Costner and the sure knowledge that you've gotten your deep shedness out into the open.

The only trouble is that you'll have missed the point. Getting things out into the open is the very opposite of what a good shed is about. A shed is about getting things into the shade, the shelter, the dark.

But commonsense won't stop the shed opportunists. Besides, careers can be made. There are big fat gold-embossed books to be sold in airports and hardware stores with titles like: *Women who Love Men who Love Sheds* or *Men are from Sheds and Women are from Somewhere Else.* Women present whole new market opportunities, too.

Sheds can resist most things but can they resist this final onslaught of new-age self-interest? Having defied consumerism, television, and heaven knows what else, the last wave could be committees of blokes in ponytails coming around to psychically realign your shed.

Come on, guys. Hands off sheds. Leave them alone now.

Jean-Paul Ferris, Darwin, Northern Territory

Like hell I will

I SAT IN THE doorway of my shed in agony. A few minutes ago I was on the roof taking down a piece of timber which I had stored there. As I turned it over I felt a spider web and saw a flaming big redback spider almost on my finger. I dropped the timber in fright, automatically took a step back and ran out of roof. I made a detour through 10 feet of airspace to the ground and landed sitting on my backside.

My missus, who was in the shed, came out and asked that foolish question that people always ask you when you have done yourself some bodily harm: "Are you hurt?"

"Of course I'm hurt!" I yelled. You can't fall 10 feet, land on your bum and not get hurt.

"I'll go and ring the doctor. Stay there," she said.

I looked at her with some disgust. "How in the hell can I move with a busted bum. Get me some medicine."

"What medicine?" she asks.

"That brown stuff you call sherry."

"Oh! I only keep it for cooking."

"And to pour it through the cook," I observed.

She went back into the shed and uncovered my plant of Tolley's Hospital Brandy . . . Gawd, she knew of my secret plant all the time. She handed me a full measure in a glass she had found with the bottle. "This will suit you better."

Mr Tolley had designed his brandy to help the needy. This was not the first time I had been in need.

"I'll go and ring the doctor; I won't be long," she said as she toddled off. I took a long swallow of my medicine. I sat there and, like a drowning man, thought of my past life and I thought of the old shed before me.

Hell! The old wreck could tell some tales. I built my house in 1954, in those years of shortages after the war. The War Service Homes mob lent me 2,750 quid (pounds to you youngsters) to build the house on land which cost me 300 greenbacks. That was all I had, so there wasn't any dough left for niceties like a shed.

My mother-in-law had a boarder, a bloke called Jimmy, and he was a real good bloke, one of the old mob. He'd break his back to help you in a time of need. Jimmy cleaned boilers for a crust and so he moved around a bit from factory to factory. At one place where he was working he discovered that the owner bloke was demolishing the property next door to extend his business. There was an old dilapidated shed down the back of the property. Jimmy put the hard word on him for the old shed and was told he could have it for nothing if he demolished it by the weekend.

Jimmy rode his bike over to my joint that night and told the missus and me of our good fortune. Whacko! You beaut, a shed at last!

He arranged with a drinking mate of his to borrow a flat-top truck. This bloke took the firm's truck home to clean and store each weekend and his boss never questioned how he used it.

As I had to work Saturday mornings, we went in the afternoon to pull it down. We pulled the iron off and knocked the frame down in record time, loaded it on the truck and brought it home to my joint. It cost me only a half a dozen bottles of beer for the truckie. Next weekend Jimmy and the bloke next door helped me assemble the shed. It cost me almost nix.

The missus came back from the 'phone and told me the doctor was on his way, but would be a while as he had to finish surgery. She had told him not to hurry as I was conscious and not too badly hurt. Struth! If an arm busted in two places, at the wrist and shoulder, and a cracked pelvis is not being badly hurt, then I don't know what is.

She poured a drop more medicine into my glass and said: "I'll have to go into the house and wait for the doctor, as he won't find you here. Will you be all right?"

I knew that I wouldn't be all right, for she took the medicine bottle with her. That's the end of that bottle I thought.

My shed. What is it? The shed is a place to park the bike and store the garden tools; and to give the cat somewhere to sleep, so she rewards you by turning it into a maternity ward. It is a place to keep the chook food and the kid's big toys. It is a household storehouse.

The shed is a man's refuge. There are times a man needs a bolt hole. Somewhere where he can escape the ear bashing he gets when he has had a night out with the boys and needs somewhere peaceful to recover and rest the throbbing pain in the old block.

The shed is a yarning place. A place where you can take a visiting mate on some pretence to tell him an off-beat story that you would not tell in polite company like the missus's. You reach under the bench to the hidden drawer and hitch out a bottle of plonk and two glasses and say: "Hey! have yer heard this one." Gawd! Have I heard and told some beauts in that old tin shed.

The shed is a thinking place. A place where a man can go and sort out serious problems, such as what to give the old girl for her birthday and how you can explain to her that you lost the 10 quid at the races that she gave you to pay the electricity bill. Believable fibs come into your head like magic in this male retreat.

I moved to take the last swig of my medicine and I looked at the old derelict. She had done me well for the last 15 years. I'll give her a reward, a coat of paint when I'm better. She deserves it.

The missus's voice interrupted my thoughts. "Doctor's here."

The quack stood and looked at me and grinned. "Fell off the roof, old boy — no wonder, it's an absolute wreck. Make him pull it down, Mrs Tamlin."

I recoiled in horror and said to myself: Pull me shed down? Pull me old mate down? Like hell I will, you stupid mug.

Ralph Tamlin, South Plympton, South Australia

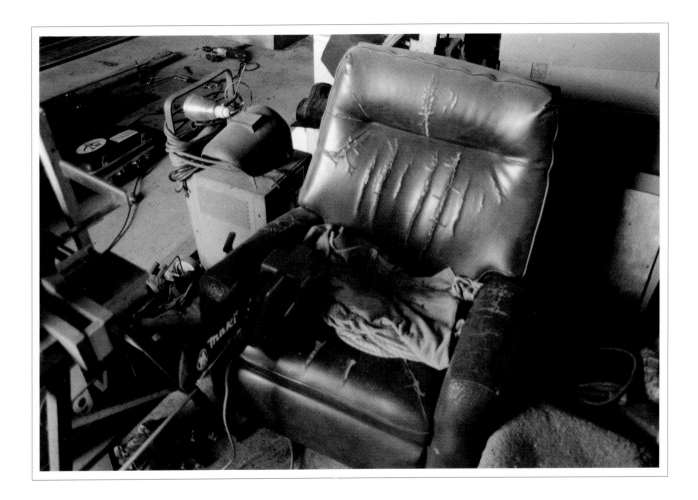

Remembering Dad

Some of these stories verge on the maudlin and sentimental, the writers recalling their fathers as men they identified very closely with the shed. A great many contributors sent in almost identical letters listing, in detail, the clutter and atmosphere of their childhood sheds, their fathers often being slightly remote figures.

What does it mean? There's something of significance here. Perhaps that communication between fathers and their children was often an uncertain dialogue, filled with spaces and pauses. Perhaps that sparse conversation was all that was necessary, minimal yet expansive in the same way that the ocean or the desert have their own beauty.

How is this changing? A good many of these writers in reflecting on their fathers show a degree of detailed insight and observation that would have been unusual "in the old days". People's expectation of fathers, these days, are that they are more articulate and expressive.

Planed all round

THE SHED WAS linked to the carport by the concrete runner with the grass centre-strip, to run the car through for the more comprehensive repair job.

The back door of the house was in an oblique alignment with the shed door. The expanse of mowed lawn and garden was the His/Hers, neutral territory between house and shed. But as a kid, it was dangerous because it was where you could be easily seen heading for the shed and be gunned down by Her, and hauled back in to do your bedroom. (Girls had to do bedrooms for some reason, boys cut the lawn edges and didn't do dishes or set tables, and it goes on and on.)

The house was Mum's lot and was about being a girl, dumb stuff — like marrying, babies, cooking and the drudgery of washing, ironing, cleaning — all of which seemed awful, except for the fence gossip (exchanges which boggled the imagination of the listening child).

The shed was the masculine territory, Dad's place for men's business. His space was potent, full of mysteries. The shed spoke of an outside world: intelligence, jobs, the workforce, politics, sport, making things and getting your hands dirty.

The shed doors were unlocked by Dad, ceremoniously on the weekends and public holidays, and in other nocturnal hours after work or after dinner — or after a blue with Mum, when he'd barricade himself in, locking the door from the inside, and whilst she howled out: "Bon, let me in", he'd plough a lump of wood through the home-made planer to drown her out. "For God's sake, woman, you drive a bloke dippy."

Nrrr Nrrr Nrrr the machine would go into the wee hours of the night — long before people complained about noise. Curls of the wooden locks fell to the floor, caught in the cobwebs, spinning, dangling. The wood stripped to clean smooth timber, weeping sap, and PAR timbers of future projects.

He would tune into the home-front bulletins (the domestic internals) via his two-way intercom connection.

As a female child I was kept on the outside of shed ceremonies but passively, in an earnest attempt to become a marginal boy, via a process of osmosis, I learnt my skills of the trade at a distance. Bandsaw cutting, framing, constructing, and the aesthetic appreciation of geometric patterns and technical illustrations were learnt through standing clear and watching, listening and smelling.

I admired the pattern of the tool board, and smelled oil, turpentine, metal shavings and the gas from the Bunsen burner. I listened to the aggressive machinery ripping, cutting, planing and sanding. I listened to the sound of football mixed with shed noise and heard the fallen silences when the game got exciting, almost as respectful as the 11th hour of Remembrance Day.

Door unlocked, lights on, radio on. His scratchy radio-mixed-machine noise irritated the ambience of Mrs Jones's backyard next door. Her Bill played golf quietly. Dad reckoned he was a bit wet and certainly under the thumb.

In the middle of a Melbourne Cup broadcast, Mrs Jones's face appeared like a twisted sandshoe over her side of the fence and told Dad where to stick his blinking machinery. With a few drinks under her belt, she'd had a gut full of his noise. You couldn't blame her really. I mean, honestly you couldn't. Nothing would stop him, especially the bellyaching of any woman (let alone from next door) who had no shed sympathy nor respect for a handyman's need to get a job finished ready for the next job.

Curious about the larger world outside the house, my father would explain scientific phenomena — about lightning and electricity and sometimes demonstrate by example with home-made scientific apparatus — or explain the mechanics of the car engine he was overhauling or the radio he was fixing.

He gave us shock therapy from some apparatus with a dirty big red-painted magnet that he'd removed from the guts of old telephone-exchange gear. "Just hang onto the two wires and I'll turn the handle."

The trips to the dump were special. With a sense of duty, Dad would brief us kids on the way to the tip and we would scavenge for the treasure, bringing more stuff home than we would drop. (There was the project: a caravan, the curved plywood type, but the most we found were parts for the chassis which became the trailer built to take more junk to the tip. Eventually it got itself a tubular framework welded up in the shed and a custom-made tarp, and the trailer was photographed being towed away by the two-toned Vauxhall on the family holiday, stuffed to the hilt.)

The tip was a takeaway feast of cryptic three-dimensional puzzles: identifying pieces, realising their potential for another use, cross-matching data, building resources, triggers for the imagination. We suffered the monologues uttered: "Waste not, want not" and "Bless this mess", and subliminally took on the cause.

Adventures to the hardware shops were the equivalent of a short-term course in museum studies, and journeys through the yellow pages of trade industries and places of supply gave you a sense of geography and lessons in orienteering with the companionable Fuller's Street Directory. The eclectic authorship of collections, discards, potential, ordering and geometry are inherent in the Fuller genes.

The mini world of valves, transistors, watch parts, photographic equipment, hardware and intrigue was closeted in the Dymo-labelled drawers of the vernacular shed. His stories of redundant technologies and private failures were in storage. Layers of the stuff. Piles of gear that no-one else wanted, but BCF knew the potentials that existed within. He was the Resourceful One, the alchemist.

It was he who saved us from the Japs. It was he who built whatever it was that saved us and gave us the day whatever it is today. He believed he was immortal and that the equipment he scavenged, and the stuff he paid for, would last forever until the end of the universe.

He built us a wooden Buffalo (packing case and calico) for Australia Day and an orb (tennis ball, cardboard and silver-frost enamel) and crown (cardboard and cotton-wool fur) for the Coronation, and taught us the respect he thought he deserved. Our dad was the cleverest. He showed us his guts, where "in the Islands" the Japs got him with a bayonet. When we bought friends to the shed, he would pull up his shirt and show the awe-filled acolytes the dirty great big umbilical scar.

When he went to the shed he wore his worst clothes (glad rags), the ones with big tears in the arse, fly buttons missing — the ones you wouldn't be seen dead in anywhere else. (As it would be at his moment of death. He arrived DOA at the hospital mortuary in his Yakkas. For his funeral, at the family's request, he was re-dressed in his best brown suit.)

Whilst he continued his nocturnal shed commitments, Mum knitted him beanie hats, in

North Adelaide footy-team colours, which protected his scalp from grazes as he dodged all the gear stacked overhead in the shed or collected oil as he lay under the old bomb doing the home maintenance on the car.

Lured by the Kingswood's greased nipples, he'd slide, in his Yakkas, under her with his glowing handyman's torch and enter the man's territory, and tinker and grunt for hours. It was always a Solvol scrub at the back-door tap after he'd been with her.

The handyman torch and extension cords trailing to the job at hand, buzzing flouros and badly tuned radio, were all part of his shed ambience.

A full bladder or the cup of tea and cheese-on-Jatz linked the house to the shed. Sometimes he was accused of "wizzing" on the grapefruit tree. She, the gardener, had a sharp sense of smell and she could discern whether it was a man's or a straying tom's, because she'd been a nurse.

The shed was his place to seek peace and solitude, a place to ponder the hypothetical and to pursue dreams.

Helen Fuller, Everard Park, South Australia

The original handyman

MY DAD WAS the original handyman, no kidding.

Anyone who remembers the heady times that heralded the early days of television might remember my dad: 1957 in Melbourne, Channel 7's "The Handyman Show" Col Burns. Forget your Tim Allens — my dad (by his own account) was the consummate home handyman. He had 'em renovating and tiling and clamping and drilling in the aisles.

He provided an excuse for thousands of males of that time to retreat to their sheds to exercise the skills and execute the projects he demonstrated with such dexterity on "The Handyman Show".

Befitting a handyman of such stature, Dad had a shed. No ordinary shed, this — it was "The Workshop". I grew up with the belief that the words "Dad" and "Workshop" were synonymous. Even now I can't hear the word without thinking of Dad.

My parents bought the house in 1955. According to Mum it was the location, but I know that Dad saw "Workshop" potential from the moment he set eyes on the garage and that was it.

My childhood memories of Dad are filled with rainy Saturday afternoons perched on a stool in the Workshop, listening to the Demons thrash 'em at the G on the old crystal radio set, watching Dad work on one of his projects. I don't remember long explanations of what he was doing, I was just seriously impressed that he knew how to do those things. Dad would always have a project on the go.

I would watch in wonderment as he clamped — there was always something in the clamp — and drilled and sawed.

There was nothing my dad couldn't fix and wasn't I impressed. He had a tool for everything and a hell of a lot of others that there was yet to be a task invented for.

We were never allowed in the Workshop unsupervised, and the one time I did go in alone I destroyed some (mind you only some) of my belief that Dad could do anything. He had a trick cup: when you took the ball out of it and put the cap back on, the ball magically reappeared. That day I found the false top in it. I never got in again alone. Anyway it just wasn't done. It was trespass.

Once Dad brought home an old telephone intercom from the office. It was supposed to be for us kids to play with, but Dad had other ideas. He connected it up between the kitchen and the Workshop; that was the last we saw of him for weeks. I think that was about the time the stretcher got set up in the Workshop. The Workshop had everything else in it, so at the time to us kids it seemed a natural progression, but in hindsight I guess it was Mum giving him the old "Workshop or me" ultimatum. Don't get me wrong; Dad adored Mum, but the Workshop was just a place he had to be. I guess he must have eventually got back into the house at night because the stretcher got packed away again.

Dad would never pay anyone to fix anything, so if it broke down it ended up the garage. Even if it didn't break down it would often end up in the garage anyway, so that Dad could pull it apart and make it work better. Never mind that it often didn't end up working better, more likely never to work again.

Dad renovated the house for nearly 40 years. I remember the bathroom renovation particularly well. It was one of the coldest winters in years and us kids were pre-school, so still bathing, not showering. Dad took out the bath and shower to line the walls. For a few days there we just had a quick wash in the sink, but when it became apparent that it was going to be some time before the renovations were complete, Mum put her foot down.

We got the shower back. Us kids thought it was great; showers were a novelty at first but a novelty that soon wore off, especially with draughts between the lining boards blustering through. Meanwhile, the bath sat in the garage for a couple of years. When we finally did get it back, nobody used it because we weren't used to baths by then.

Dad was introduced to the concept of skylights around my tenth birthday. He started systematically installing them that summer throughout the house. Fortunately it was a slow process because by winter they were leaking everywhere and Dad was stopped in his tracks at skylight number three, by Mum juggling saucepans full of rainwater through the house. The following winter I remember sitting down to the kitchen table for Sunday lunch when Dad joined us via the skylight; fortunately he wasn't hurt, though the same couldn't be said for the roast. Covered in plaster dust and gravy, Dad retired to the Workshop to clamp something.

Years passed and the Workshop filled with even more amazing tools, more broken articles awaiting salvation from the rubbish heap.

Dad got sick, developing Alzheimer's disease after Mum passed away. He kept up with repairing this and fixing that, almost living out of his beloved Workshop. But the problem was that this insidious disease made all that drilling and clamping and fixing and repairing unsafe. Dad had to move.

It was a unit to start with, not far away, but it didn't have a workshop. Some days he had trouble recalling my name but he could never forget how to get home to the Workshop. Tools started appearing at the unit. I found screwdrivers in the cutlery drawer, drills in the bathroom cabinet. Dad couldn't drive but he was slowly transporting his beloved Workshop, tool by tool, to the unit. We tried locking the Workshop but he used the tools in the garage to break in. We felt like we were cutting off his lifeline.

Dad moved to a nursing home. He passed away last October. Thinking about it now I wish it had've been in the Workshop.

I inherited the house; it had been so successfully renovated in those 40 years that it had to be demolished. That hurt. But the garage and Workshop stayed. We built a new house around the old garage but the Workshop stayed as it always was. It cost us, but how could I demolish it? Anyway what would I do with all the tools and "handy things" in the Workshop?

We had a baby son three months before Dad died and he will grow up with the Workshop just like I did. What he wants to do with it is up to him, meanwhile the clamp still clamps and the drill still drills and it's still my dad's Workshop.

Lisa Burns, Burwood, Victoria

Shoe polish and stout

Method of making Leather Boot Laces. Pull the leather against a knife stuck in the bench.

IN THE DAYS when most shoes were made of leather and were expected to be kept brightly polished, Percy spent every Sunday morning polishing the family shoes in his shed. Whilst he did not go to church, keeping shoes in good order was close enough to religion for Percy.

In those days shoes had to last and Percy made sure that the family shoes were in good repair. Gluing a new rubber sole onto the slightly worn leather sole, he would cut around the edges to maintain the correct shape and then tack a metal tip on to the heel and toe to save wear and tear. None of his family's shoes ever saw the inside of a shoe-repair shop, not while Percy had a shoe last and supplies in his shed to do the job.

A thorough and energetic polishing followed, with the aid of Kiwi Shoe Polish. The resulting gleaming shoes were proudly worn by all three generations of the family.

Percy was a perfectionist with a meticulously tidy shed. Yet the shed was full of secrets: ancient documents, books and photographs, letters and other memorabilia, stories about ancestors and skeletons in the cupboard.

But Percy's biggest secret was his empty bottles which had contained Woodroofe's Sarsaparilla. Percy over-imbibed. He liked his pint of beer or stout; in fact he liked it so much that he often arrived home late from work walking a crooked line.

This was not appreciated by his wife, who had a horror of alcohol and would not have allowed it in the house or even through the gate if she had known it was in Percy's bag. So Percy hid his contraband Cooper's Stout in the shed and, when the time was right, he would transfer it into his sarsaparilla bottles. When his daughters' suitors came to visit, he would entertain them with the contents.

How did he keep his Cooper's Stout cold? After transferring it into his sarsaparilla bottles, with their screw tops tightly sealed, he would deposit one on the ice in the ice chest on the closed-in back verandah nearby. There were no such luxuries as a spare fridge in the shed in those days. Another bottle was kept standing by in the shed as a replacement. The empty stout bottles would be wrapped in newspaper and deposited amongst the rubbish in the bin. Everyone was happy.

In some ways Percy's shed was his religion: where else could he go to meditate on life? He could only go where all sane men go when they need comfort and peace — to the shed, of course, and maybe sit on a box and read a book.

Percy was my dad.

Shirley Flavel, Strathalbyn, South Australia

Jack of all trades, master of none

DAD WAS A QUIET, secretive man, very modest but very intelligent, too. He was stocky but deceptively quick on his feet — he'd been a champion runner in his youth.

His family had been farriers and he had acquired their affinity for working with metal. He seemed to be able to do anything and everything. A jack of all trades and master of none, as he described himself.

In the summer he always wore a wharfie's singlet and pants, and a pair of sandals with socks underneath. In the winter he added a flannelette shirt and a cardigan, accompanied by a peaked cap. He didn't care about clothes. He would even use the clothes he was wearing to clean up oil spills and whatever.

Dad was always in the shed. You could always find him there, whistling and smoking. The smoking was a ritual. He would come in, slowly roll a ragged smoke, then pause and consider his next move. It was a kind of short period of acclimatisation, of paying respect to the spirit of the shed.

Dad never mastered the art of rolling your own. His fags were always wet, limp, thin jobs hanging out of his mouth, with a few loose strands protruding from the end like a strange catfish. Half of it went up in flames when he lit it and what was left he blew out whistling. I could never workout why the hell he smoked.

The shed was Dad's domain. He never let you forget that it was some kind of a holy place. Touching was not permitted, looking was acceptable but questions were to be kept to a minimum. He'd been a member of the Druids when he was younger — maybe that was something to do with why he liked that sort of atmosphere.

Naturally, being an inquisitive child, I asked a lot of questions as to what he was making. He must have made a staggering number of wigwams for gooses' bridles.

In fact he made just about everything we could possibly need. Stuff for Mum, toys for us, even his own tools, turning them on the lathe, as he couldn't afford to buy them. He made beautiful, practical things; but what was more important was the joy that he made them with, through his beautiful hands and his love of life and us.

You can tell if a man has a shed. He's got a look about him. He knows he can create, can do things that other men can't; a there's a certain sort of confidence and pride. He doesn't run down the shop to buy a new one; instead it's give it here, I'll fix it. He wants to know the guts of the matter, how it works, how to make it work again.

That was Dad. He knew the mechanics of the workings of life and it rubbed off on us all.

Some men climb Mt Everest. Dad had a shed. There was no difference to me.

Jill Dingley, Aldgate, South Australia

It might come in handy one day

THE DOORS OF the shed were held open by two pieces of packing-case timber, neatly trimmed to a point with the tomahawk. The dull green ivy which covered the rotting paling fence alongside had started to curl around one door, its fingers examining the strokes of colour. Bill cleaned his paint brushes on the inside of the doors before immersing the brushes in a jar of turps. The jars sat in the shadows in the shed, on the top shelf. As the turps evaporated, the brushes slowly bent on their black bristles — but Bill said they'd come in handy one day.

The shed doors had long swipes of cream and green paint from the kitchen, canary yellow from the bathroom, silverfrost from the downpipes and brick red from the galvanised roof. A repainted second-hand Malvern Star bicycle provided red, white and blue criss-crosses. Bill had brought the bike home from the auction mart where he worked. I'd always wanted a Speedwell.

The morning of my eighth birthday Uncle Bill stood just outside the shed at the top of the driveway. He held the back of the seat and the mudguard as I clenched the rubber grips. "Promise you won't let go!" I said, but he gave me a push off and somehow I wobbled down the driveway and crashed into the ivy next to red iron front gate. "Now you can ride a two-wheeler," he said. "You can keep it in the shed."

The shed was Bill's haven. His wife, Madge, didn't go near it. Along one wall was a bench where Bill kept a small guillotine for shaving his plugs of tobacco, an iron shoe last with three different-sized feet and one heel for shoe repairs, and a huge square tin of honey. Above were shelves which held steels to sharpen knives. The scraping rhythm always set my teeth on edge. There were hammers and awls and sheets of warm-smelling leather and pungent rubber to make soles and heels and special smelly glue and tins of black tacks and a tack hammer to attach them to our worn shoes.

There were jars of galvanised roofing nails and fencing nails; tins of black and brown and mahogany Nugget shoe polish and methylated spirits and rags and brushes to clean and polish shoes for Sunday and part-empty tins of paint which might get used one day. In the corner, Queensland Blue pumpkins and bags of potatoes from the garden were stored to be used in the cold winter months.

Along the opposite wall, above the bikes and push lawnmower, were things that hung on four-inch nails. The coal scuttle hung above the pile of coke in the summer. There were fox and rabbit skins stretched over U-shaped pieces of wire; a hessian water bag; the hessian grass catcher; spare wheels for the old pram; bicycle wheels and a rusting bike frame.

There were tea chests and pieces of timber, an old chest of drawers and shelves which might come in useful one day. The old meat cooler, which had been replaced by the ice chest, stood in the corner.

There were rolls of chicken wire and an old brooder, hedge clippers, forks and spades and edge trimmers, a wheelbarrow, a pickaxe, a mattock, a grass roller and a crowbar and a set of ancient scales with weights.

Empty wheat bags from the corner pile could be used to keep your head and shoulders dry when you wanted to play in the lucerne tree in the chook yard. You could pretend to be the caped crusader. You just poked the bag in the corner, put it on your head and tied it around your neck with a piece of twine from the shelf.

The gleanings from the bran, pollard and wheat bags attracted mice and rats which scuttled into the wood heap when you approached. Bill set mouse and rat traps, carefully burning the cheddar before setting the spring. We'd check the traps on Saturdays and discuss the length of rats' tails.

I never went into the back of the shed. There were no windows in the thick timber walls. It was always dark in the back even with the doors propped open and I was scared that Something lurked behind the wood pile. The rafters were hung with old spiders' webs thick with dust, and bunches of brown Spanish onions. The floor was hard-packed dirt dotted with the landings of flying red gum or white box woodchips waiting to be gathered and rolled in newspaper to start the chip bath heater and cosy stove.

Near the chopping block were the dried rusty blood stains told of the countless black Australorps, white Leghorns and Rhode Island reds which had come to the end of their egg-laying days. Sometimes the body ran around and around looking for its head, and once my cousin Ted put my head on the chopping block and said he was going to chop off my head.

The chooks were hung upside down from the ceiling to drain the blood and then they were plunged into a galvanised tub of boiling water to make them easy to pluck. We rested the chooks on one block of wood and sat on the other, pulling the feathers back up the body.

Sometimes I collected the wing feathers to make an Indian headdress and I'd holler and whoop chasing the chooks around the yard. Bill plunged his hand inside the chook and dragged out its innards. He carefully cleaned the craw of pebbles and unused wheat and this and the other giblets were boiled in the stockpot which always stood on the back of Madge's black Bega fuel stove. I often claimed the legs and enjoyed sucking the jelly-like goodness from the clawed feet.

Madge stuffed the chooks with egg, breadcrumbs and shallots, parsley and rosemary from the garden and roasted them with three vegetables and gravy for Sunday dinner.

Before Bill began his chores early on a Saturday morning we'd sit in the shed on our respective blocks of wood reserved for the purpose. I'd check the hollow centre to make sure no spiders were lurking before I sat down. Bill would give a groan or two and his knees would crack in protest. The chooks in the yard behind the shed would begin clucking as soon as they heard us. He'd take his rose briar pipe from his Saturday cardigan pocket, hold the bowl and gently scrape it clean with a pen knife, upending and tap tap tapping it clean.

He'd take a thumb and finger full of strands from his brown leather tobacco pouch and massage them in the palm of his hand as we breathed in the frosty morning.

I'd amuse myself drawing stick figures in the dirt with a piece of kindling split from packing cases as he'd carefully pack the tobacco in the pipe bowl, pushing it down with his thumb and finally tamping it with a Federal matchbox. I'd always stop to watch him strike the match and light and suck and light and suck until it was just right.

He'd tell me a yarn. My favourite was that if you were confronted by a taipan in the bush all you had to do was take off your hat and throw it just in front of the snake and it wouldn't take its eyes off the hat and you could kill it or just walk away.

"That's enough yarning for today," he would say. He'd go and get the small kettle full of hot water from the kitchen stove and we'd walk through the gate to the little shed in the chook yard. To save him bending double, Bill would send me in and instruct me in the makings of hot mash for the chooks. Take two large tins of pollard and one of bran. Mix well together in the old enamel dish then add the hot water, mix again and let it stand for a minute or two. The steam would rise and the chooks would begin fighting to stake their claim. Sometimes I'd pinch a mouthful when Bill wasn't looking.

In the late afternoon the chooks were fed wheat and sometimes corn that Bill had grown in the paddock up the back. We'd prepare it in the morning, peeling off the leaves and drooping brown tassels and prising the kernels out with our thumbs. Then he'd change his clothes for work, put bicycle clips on his trousers and freewheel down the Lord's Place hill on his bicycle.

On weekdays promptly at 6 pm, and 1 pm on Saturdays, the taxi truck called for him at Nookie Farrell's Great Western Hotel and drove him and his bicycle back up the hill.

Bill was the nearest I ever had to a father. He'd married my aunt in 1943. My mother was getting a divorce and was going to put me in a home. "Over my dead body," Bill said, and I moved to live with them in Orange.

He loved Bob Menzies, SP betting, listening to the races on the wireless on Saturday afternoons, smoking his pipe, reading the *Herald*, the back shed and his job as an auctioneer.

I left Orange when I was 15 and I only saw him once after that. He got bowel cancer and couldn't get up to the shed. But I can still see him sharpening the carving knives on the grinding stone in the chook yard. He'd pedal and spit on the stone as it turned and he'd grind first one side and then the other. He'd sit in the shed giving each knife a final hone with the sharpening steel and take out his pipe and tell a lonely little kid about Bob Menzies and how to escape from taipans.

Rae Luckie, Springwood, New South Wales

Charles's journey

MY FATHER CHARLES was born in a small village in Lebanon and, although he lived 70 years in Australia, he never really left his birthplace.

He arrived here by sea as a seven year old wearing the simple, flowing robes of the Arab and remembered looking in amazement over the railing of the boat as it pulled into Fremantle Harbour at a strange sight — a man in trousers riding a bicycle.

This is an enduring story and an indelible image of my father — as a little olive-skinned boy, undoubtedly barefoot, with jet-black hair, standing on tiptoe and drinking in this scene with a mix of wonder and great excitement. It was here also he literally drank in another new experience — swallowing water from a glass.

His memories of Lebanon and the village he left were sparse — he remembered sharing the warmth of their house with the sheep and the goats in the winter, the ride in an open-topped car from his village down to the port — but it was the texture of his childhood he carried with him vividly until his death.

He remembered, for instance, the smell of the walnut leaves from the tree at the bottom of the village, and so at our homes he would plant a walnut and treat it as if it were the only tree in the garden. He had a habit of unconsciously plucking a leaf from the tree and crushing it between his thumb and forefinger, releasing the pungent oil, then sniffing the leaf deeply, as if trying to inhale his birthplace deep into his soul.

And he remembered vividly the smell of his grandfather — a sweet smell of sweat on the clothes and in the hollow of his throat and the nape of his neck, a scent which no doubt triggered memories for my father of hugging and snuggling into his grandfather as a young boy.

A few months after his death, my mother gave me one of my father's jackets — a black and grey sportscoat that had been hanging in the bedroom wardrobe with the rest of his things. My father did not believe in wasting money on clothes, but he always invested in good-quality coats and English shoes. When I got home I unwrapped the jacket and pushed the material to my face and breathed in the scent of my father, clinging to it as he clung to the scent of his birthplace, his walnut trees, his grandfather.

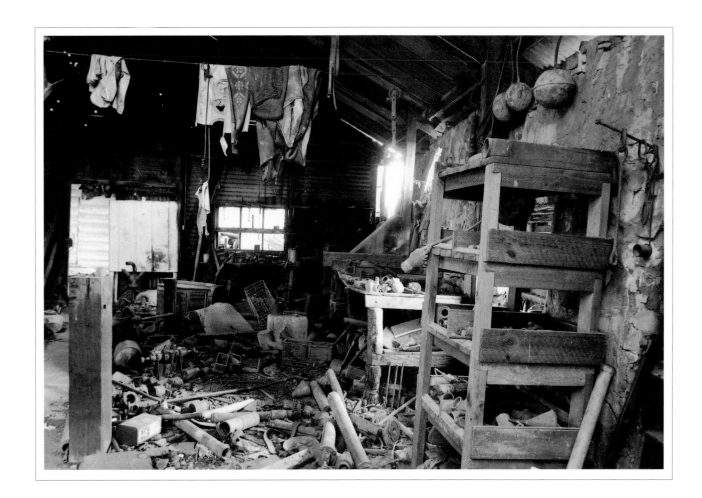

The jacket's been dry-cleaned now, and so for me the only tangible reminder of my father's presence is trapped in his shed. The smell of sawn wood, sawdust, wood shavings in the planes, shellac and metho — these are the indelible imprints of my father's life. Dad was a carpenter and polisher and while the smell of the chemical lacquers and thinners were the bane of his working life, he loved working with shellac, the ancient combination of beetle shell and metho which seals the grain of good timber, locking in a honeyed warmth.

The shed is in fact little more than a galvanised iron lean-to, tacked onto the side of a single iron garage. It has windows down one side, with wheat bags for curtains. Every nook and cranny, every hole in the wood and every tuck of corrugated iron, has a tool or device stashed into it. An old wire bed-frame, the sort you still find in country pubs, is suspended from the ceiling, acting as a shelf for more tools, lengths of wood and assorted oddments.

The only concession to entertainment is a valve radio, hooked up to the one power point, which also serves the other concession to the electric era — a sawbench. The saw is a triumph of she'll-be-right ingenuity — it is mounted on a wood base with lawnmower wheels, a drill chuck has been welded on one spinning end and a car jack has been bolted to the side for vertical adjustment. No chair, no dartboard, no fridge but, inexplicably, a big yet unused Pye phonogram occupies one end of the shed.

The workbench is a beauty — it's made out of slabs of hardwood, which have been chipped, chiselled and worn smooth with half a century of use. It is deeply stained and shiny from years of shellac spills and accumulated layers of glue. Dad turned out some amazing creations and restorations from his few square metres of shed — chests of drawers, bookcases, little sets of tables and chairs for his grandchildren. They were made to go the distance, too.

In his youth, he and his brother, Frank, ran a small furniture factory. They made ladder-back kitchen chairs which had a distinctive, subtle design. Recently I was talking to someone who bought one of their kitchen suites in the 1950s — it's still going strong, now in his daughter's kitchen.

Dad's trademark was a rose-colored wood stain, worked in with a bundle of old woollen socks until it came up soft, warm and the colour of black–red cherries.

Dad's tools had always been beyond limits when we were kids, and so they held a special fascination — the metre-long plane he used for levelling doors, the chisels, the cute little tack hammer, the enormous clamps, big enough to squeeze together an entire tabletop. After his death, it was surprising to find that his tools had aged with him — like my father, they looked fine at a quick glance, but deep down they simply wore out. The saw handles have been repaired over and over again, the chisels are worn and their handles held together with hose clamps, the superb planes are now battered.

Whenever Dad picked up a piece of wood he would instinctively rub it with his hands and then, unconsciously, bring it up to his nose and smell it. Baltic, cedar, oak, red pine — he could pick a fine wood from a dud plank of meranti by its characteristic smell.

Sometimes, it's all we have left.

Matthew Abraham, Hyde Park, South Australia

Shed therapy

I WANT TO TELL you about the power of shed therapy.

At the age of 63, my father had a brain haemorrhage, which caused deficits to his short-term memory and made walking difficult. The medical advice was that he would more or less be a vegetable and should go home and lead a very quiet life.

As a determined family we worked on him day and night, doing the physio and pepping him up with books and videos of his favourite subject: gyrocopters.

His shed was filled with bits and pieces of gyrocopters as well as fridges, a relic of his engineering profession.

When we were advised to put him in a nursing home, we decided against it and knew that there was only one place, one thing that would rehabilitate him — his shed!

His passion was his best therapy. No jigsaw puzzles or bed exercises for him. Real tasks and real machines that would give his memory a challenge, piece by piece.

Against his doctor's advice we let him loose to fiddle with electricity.

It was do or die! And he loved it. He went back to his gyrocopters and his fridges. His mates came around, spending hours with him, reinforcing his memory, making him laugh.

At times he'd use the wrong tool, or put tools down and spend hours searching for them. But it worked. He eventually went back to his old job. It wouldn't have been possible without that shed and all the wondrous things in it.

I've got a shed, too, complete with drills, jigsaws and sanders. Yes, a woman with a shed! With a few tips from my father I've just built a sleep-out from scratch, from joists and frames up.

No matter what I do build, it'll be done in my shed, with the handmade tools that have come from my Grandpa Smith via my father.

Jan Hill, Mt Barker, South Australia

Funny Business

There's all sorts of dodgy stuff that people get up to in sheds. There's a kind of semi-criminality about a shed, a hint of the illegitimate. Some of these activities are illegal. Some are fun. Some are most definitely not socially acceptable. All part of the shady business . . .

Sheduction

BEING THE SON of a lifelong petrolhead, it was inevitable that I would follow in my father's footsteps. I virtually grew up in the garage. Billycarts at age 8, minibikes at 10 and my first car, bought in a collection of boxes, at 13.

Dad reasoned that it would keep me off the streets. He was quite right but it also meant that I never got around to learning the social graces. For some reason, girlfriends seemed to tire very quickly of spending their time working on my old Jag. They soon lost interest.

Then, at a mate's nineteenth birthday bash (held in his dad's shed, of course), I met Jenny. Not only was she dead-set gorgeous but she was mad keen on old sports cars. We hit it off right away. She was a pretty good mechanic, too, and even had her own overalls.

This was serious.

After a few months we were inseparable. The Jag was almost finished and, to celebrate, we planned a big night out at a swank restaurant.

On Saturday afternoon, as I was putting a few final touches on the car, I saw the telltale sign of fresh oil on the floor under the gearbox. Oh, no. There was nothing to be done but to put her up on the stands and get to work.

Seven o'clock came and I was still trying to get the new seal in the back of the box. Jen arrived in the sexiest little black number you'll ever see and is, to say the least, not impressed. After a heated exchange (our very first), she stormed off, vowing not to come back.

If you've ever tried to work on a car when you're mad as hell then you'll know that the only thing you're going to achieve is skinned knuckles.

By 10.30 I was still trying to put the tailshaft back in, when, to my surprise, Jen came back and asked if I wanted a hand. I could see from under the car that the black dress was gone, replaced by the familiar red cuffs of her overalls. I crawled out from under the car and to my surprise and delight the red windcheater she normally wore under the red bib and brace overalls was nowhere to be seen.

The effect was breathtaking. Up until now, we'd only engaged in the odd kiss and cuddle but this was an entirely different box of nuts and bolts.

The tailshaft never did get put back in that night. However, the bonnet got a hell of a workout. Three months later we got married and six months after that our daughter was born. We've got our own shed now and in the 16 years since then we've built some great cars in it. Each one of them has had the red overall treatment. Some of these cars have been real works of art but I doubt if we'll ever build anything as awesome as the little girl we created that night.

It was only recently I found out that it was Jen's mum who suggested that if she wanted to catch a fish then she had to go fishing where the fish liked to swim. I don't know if she suggested what bait to use but God bless her wisdom anyway.

John Van Workum, Doncaster East, Victoria

The shed for all reasons

My husband had a shed.

He used it for everything. He brewed his beer in it, put Kromide soles on all our shoes, sharpened knives on his emery wheel, mixed paints and, after a blue with me (which was quite often), slept in it.

We had a small cottage and, as our three daughters grew up, our house seemed to get smaller. Our privacy shrunk with it; there seemed to be no escape from them. So we often met in the shed. We devised a system — a wink and a certain nod of the head in the direction of the shed. One of us would go up there and the other would follow in about five minutes.

Many a pleasant time was spent in the shed, with the moon shining through the door. I got to learn a lot about the stars, in more ways than one.

However, one night when the girls and I were watching television, someone said: "Where's Dad?"

"I don't know," I said, but I realised he'd been gone for quite a while. Then it hit me. My God! The shed!

I rushed up the yard and there he was, sitting stark naked in the wheelbarrow, the moon shining brightly on him.

I nearly fell over laughing but he didn't see the funny side of it at all.

"Bloody man's nearly frozen!" he said grumpily. "Didn't you see me nod at you?"

When our youngest daughter was 10 years old we had a fine healthy son. Even though I was only 33 years old and my husband 36, the girls said we were too old.

They often whispered between themselves as to how we could have done it without them knowing and how could we, at our ages, still do such things.

Now after 47 years of marriage and as great-grandparents, we often look back at our shed days and reminisce.

Elizabeth Fredericks, Bateau Bay, New South Wales

The flying shed

JOE'S SHED HAS presence.

It's modelled on those gleaming galvanised-iron barns that grow in industrial estates in Australia's far-flung suburbs. Except that Joe's shed sits in the back corner of a quarter-acre block in an inner-city suburb.

The double roller-door entrance makes it expansive, especially when opened. Inside, the shed is half workshop and half warehouse.

The workshop is moist looking, much like someone with dark unwashed hair or wearing a good dose of gel or old-style Brylcream. The warehouse side is dry, dusty and cluttered with potentially useful bits of building material and assorted furniture.

Each item has its own story, a secret it shares only with Joe. Joe says he keeps them just in case but I've a suspicion that sentiment plays a part.

Occasionally necessity targets one of the items and Joe feels all the effort and foresight is vindicated. It doesn't matter that it would have been quicker to go to the hardware shop for that elusive dynabolt instead of turning the shed upside down in frustration until it was found.

The workshop is a panorama of tools, equipment, car parts and machinery. A traumatised car and disembodied motor bike wait, centre stage, for surgery. The workshop's altar, the bench, seems to be always fully occupied. Above it, mechanical tools graded on the wall give an appearance of order and proficiency. There is no such system under the bench or for the parts loitering around the floor, waiting patiently to be attached.

But today Joe is not hurrying. He has declared it clean-up day.

Time to take stock, replace, reorder, reassess and plan the next move. He empties an old saucepan of degreasing fluid, cleans the brush and finds a spot for them under the bench. He hunts down stray spanners, rewinds cords and removes rubbish. As he cleans and categorises he also reacquaints himself with the contents and again is master.

He knows where everything is and everything is where it should be. Joe is in control again and he can start afresh. The clutter has disappeared from the workshop and from his mind. The achievement spurs him on to tackle the warehouse side, separated from the rest of the shed by strategically placed cupboards and shelves.

He is just about to make a move when Club calls.

Never knew his real name. He was introduced as Club, was always referred to as Club and will always be Club. The name's origin has been lost in time.

Like many of Joe's friends, Club bypasses the house and heads for the shed if signs suggest it's occupied. As always, he calls Joe by his initials. Could be very American except there's more warmth to it.

"JB, you in there?"

He pretty well knows Joe is in there. The question is more hello than uncertainty.

"Come in, Club." Joe picks Club's gruff but authoritative voice instantly.

Club's come at a good time. It's obvious that Joe is pottering about, which leaves room for a break. Always sociable, Joe doesn't need prodding. He first spars with Club.

"You're a bit of a shark, Club. How much did you end up paying that guy for his computer or did you talk him into giving it to you for nothing?"

Club swallows it.

"It was more than two years old, JB! That's ancient for computers."

"Yeah, but you offered him a third of what he wanted."

"I was only looking after my interests, JB," Club responds defensively.

"Anyway, shall we celebrate with a beer or a bong?"

"Do we have to choose?"

Joe gets the message and heads for the house to fetch the beer.

Club makes the other preparations. He knows where the stuff is. His thick large fingers take a delicate pinch of the dried leaves from their plastic pouch. He crumbles the marijuana into fine bits and loads the makeshift water-filter pipe. The brass burner gives a touch of class to the milk bottle.

Joe's back with the beer and watches Club's meticulous preparations. They laugh. At each other or at the anticipated high? It's not clear. They joke about who goes first. It's a ritual. They've done it many times before and are on familiar ground. Soon Club will have forgotten all about the woes of being a small-time contractor, about his wife expecting him home doing something useful and about lost chances.

For Joe it's the chase of another good time. The host prepares to go first but a voice calls out.

It's Dom, laconic easy-going Dom. He had gone to Club's to borrow his electric plane and the trail led him to Joe's.

Dom knew what Club, Joe and the shed added up to. If he was as sure of the night's lotto numbers he'd be a rich man. It was Saturday afternoon. And, like many other Saturday afternoons, all circumstances and all roads led to Joe's shed. And Dom wasn't going to miss out. He laughed, they all laughed. It was infectious and natural and nothing to do with the stuff.

"You were going to go without me, weren't you?" he accused.

"Well we didn't have enough for a party you know," Joe joked. "This stuff is hard to come by."

Soon they were in good spirits. Rude people would say they were high and out of their brains. But they were in the shed again, away from the real routine. Prodding pressures disappeared with each puff and life was as it should be — relaxed and good humoured.

The shed had few comforts, it was not home and it definitely was not stately. Yet it had status. It harboured high moments, deep in the backyard, away from curious eyes.

They were flying high in the shed, for moments that would soon disappear, until next time.

Cicciu Scrivi, Hobart, Tasmania

Sprung

FIVE YEARS AGO my husband almost gave up smoking. He came to dislike the smell of smoke in the house and moved his "coffin nails" to the garage, were they joined his wintertime supply of bulk-purchase port wine.

Whilst we both enjoy beer and wine with our meals, he is a chronic snorer and, following medical advice, had to cut down even more on smoking and not drink alcohol after 7.30 pm.

Then one winter's night a couple of years ago, I heard a strange choking, gagging noise coming from the garage. It was similar to those monster noises in horror movies — something like the evil spirit in *The Exorcist*.

The husband came out clutching his throat. "Quick, quick, I've swallowed a cockroach and it's stuck halfway down my throat! I can feel its legs moving!"

The husband had been sprung.

He'd been sneaking a smoke and a little glass of port in the dark and had disposed of a contented cockroach sleeping off the dregs of the Old Tawny.

It was eventually dislodged with much drama and howls of revulsion and disgust.

Somehow the story got out about the funny (well, I thought so) incident and he was referred to as "The Roach" at golf for months afterwards.

Laraine Booker, Warradale, South Australia

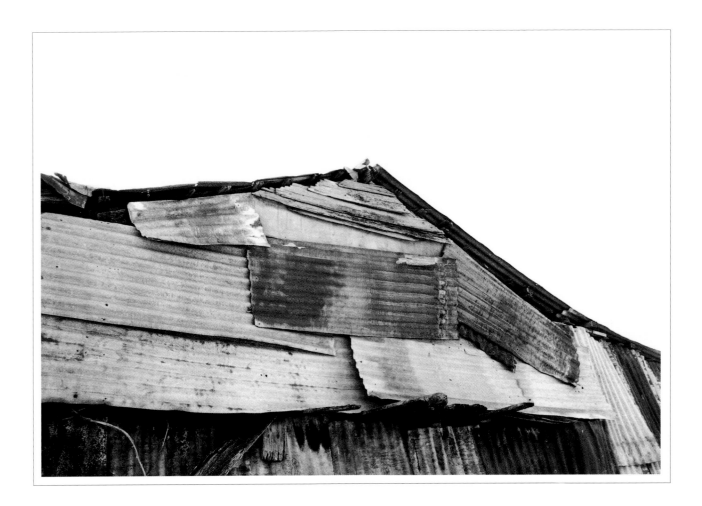

Loss

Whether it is in disappearing traditions, lost friends or the loss of the freedom of childhood or of a more innocent period of Australia's history, loss is a common theme amongst the contributions to this book.

The day of the pig

TWO MORE DROPS of blood and the saucepan was full. Nonna expertly emptied it into a bucket and carried the swirling fluid to the sink. The blood continued to drip noisily into the saucepan.

The cock crowed but the working day had already begun.

Hanging from the galvanised-iron roof, the carcass gently swayed, forcing a slight moan from the wooden rafters. One half of the pig fixed its glassy stare at the other half across the room. The eeriness and the heavy smell of death was broken only by the sounds of the couple's preparation as their 60-year-old bodies worked with amazing strength and agility in memory of the old days.

As the light filtered into the room, helping hands began to arrive: dutiful sons and daughters coming to continue the traditions they were born into. The shed came alive with the yearly killing of the pig.

To others this tradition would have appeared barbarous but for those within it was a way of life. The fact they made the products themselves was perhaps more admirable and natural in comparison to those who bought their animal parts from the supermarket, neatly packaged and indistinguishable from the original animal form.

Years of struggle through poverty had taught Nonno and Nonna to appreciate the simple things in life. Food was important. The pig killing reflected this; to the family, it was an artform. The skill lay in finding a use for every part of the carcass. Nothing was spared or wasted. Generations of rural poverty in southern Italy and hunger during the war-ridden years had taught them to live this way. And so they continued to catch every drop of blood to make the chocolate and blood delicacy that was a favourite of the children but which outsiders found so distasteful. Intestines were soaked and blown up like party balloons to become sausage skin, and bones gave flavour to soups and other dishes.

As the morning wore on, more of the family would arrive. The brigade of children added to the commotion. After an obligatory kiss on the cheek to the heads of the family, the grandchildren ran from the stench and went to play in the concrete jungle outside. Every now and then the oldest ones would be called in to carry out some chore. After Nonna gave the orders in her native tongue they'd turn to their parents for a translation into their own native tongue. Bursting into the house to fetch some dish, they'd feel uncomfortable with the silence. The house was always dark and quiet. The lounge room, dining room, even the kitchen, usually a focal point for the average Italian family, stood like a memorial. The house symbolised Nonno and Nonna's new life in Australia and all the things they never had in Italy. But it was hard to become accustomed to these things. Everyone was outside in the shed, always in the shed. It was there they lived, breathed, grew and worked. It was their culture and their heritage.

The shed was closer to how Nonno and Nonna had lived in the village. Everyone together in the one room. But even the shed was more elaborate than its Italian counterpart. Gas stove, stainless-steel sink, fridge, pantry and even a couple of lounge chairs in the corner.

The only approved break was lunchtime. Eating together was part of the ritual. Space was cleared at the workbench, a converted table-tennis table. It had once been a Christmas present for Nonno and Nonna's two youngest; but after six months Nonno and Nonna, realising its potential, claimed it for themselves. Work was more important than leisure.

It was all they knew. Having worked all their lives, the only force that could slow them down was old age and they worked to defy that too. The children had long given up hope for themselves, and in turn for their own children, of ever reclaiming the toy.

The shed fell quiet as the family refuelled for the afternoon shift. Some stood while others sat around the table, but their cheeks bulged unanimously as they chewed on food that had been made in the shed on other days. Every day they enjoyed the fruits of their labour. The children swung their legs on the chairs as their jaws wrestled the tough home-baked bread. Already they had become used to the softness of factory bread. Change had crept into the family stronghold with the new generation. It was hard to envisage them living the old ways. Would they perform the same rituals? They'd dream about them but wouldn't be able to maintain them. They lived in a different world; the traditions wouldn't come naturally. The taste of the fresh wood-oven baked bread and the smell of Nonno's wine would fade into memory. Lunch ended and the work resumed. Someone should have encouraged the children to stay, watch, help and learn. Instead they were allowed to escape back into the outside world.

Dealing with the pig was a long and laborious task. Working ceased only with increasing darkness and the approach of another mealtime. However, the huge job of cleaning up still remained. Nonno and Nonna had turned that into an artform too. Neatness symbolised beauty and, while wealth was never within their reach, they tried to remain clean. It was part of their working-class pride. In contrast to countless Aussie sheds that lay in disarray, the cleanliness of Nonno and Nonna's shed was matched only by the amazing purity of the house. Surfaces were scrubbed vigorously, a mountain of growing suds sterilised dishes. Even the cement was hosed down until it was fit to perform surgery upon.

Nonno was the last to leave the shed. Before he turned out the light from the naked bulb, his eyes roamed one more time around the room. He did a quick count of the piles of chops and sausages sitting on the table, ready to be distributed amongst the family. As he left the darkened shed, the image of sausages swinging from wooden rafters filled his mind.

Marina Barbaro, Mile End, South Australia

Shedworld

IF YOU WERE a kid around Rosehill in the 1950s, the thing that filled you with the greatest horror was not the nuclear arms race or the attitude of white Australians to coloured people. The most piteous spectacle that could meet your eyes was a boring, hygienic, tidy shed.

A real shed leaked. The roofing iron was rusted through and the guttering hung loose. It did not have proper doors because it was more of a lean-to than a garage. The only light filtered in through a dirty window, through cracks in the walls which were often grey palings, or — when emergencies demanded — came from a portable globe with wire protection and rubber handle, powered by an extension cord running from the laundry. Dark corners were essential to the sense of mystery surrounding the tin trunks and cabinets therein.

Concrete floors were a real disappointment. A true shed smelled of damp earth, clay, and rodents' droppings. Concrete just soaked up oil, and chooks could never scratch around and make dustbath hollows in concrete.

The best sheds were swathed in choko vines and some had pumpkins drying on top. Tendrils crept and curled under the roof, vying with spider webs for space in the days before people became paranoid poison-sprayers.

The sheds around Rosehill were organic, special ecosystems, practically living things in their own right. They made their own sounds — creaking iron expanding in the heat or a loose sheet flapping in the breeze, the wind whistling through cracks, the crunch of pebbles under your shoes, the echo of your voice or your father's hammering — these were all distinctive and individual.

But above all else hung the smells, most of which were associated with the way people then understood what was masculine: strong smells, weekend smells shut in to stew during the week, smells which rose on the fumes from deadly liquids like turps and kerosene, smells of dry powders waiting to be mixed for use in the garden, smells of insect sprays and fertilisers, linseed oil and other preserving and polishing agents, oily rags and drying newsprint.

There was one shed where a rich kid lived. It had a loading dock which added another dimension to games, but it was a rare event to be permitted inside. Terry, the rich kid, was away at school a lot and rarely mixed with the locals. He was troubled about something, something about his parents, and made protests in odd ways.

Once when I was admiring his shed, which was, sadly, always empty, Terry dropped his pants and shat a turd onto the loading dock. He kept on talking about other things, as though this were entirely normal behaviour. Perhaps it was. There seemed to be other, desiccated offerings on this altar-like platform. Suddenly the shed smelled earthy, imbued with the steaming stench of excrement, more like animal manure in a stable than the smells you got from toilets or from foetid classrooms just after lunch on a summer's day. That was the first time that it occurred to me that dung could be healthy, or that scats could be used to diagnose disease.

The greatest thing about sheds was that they were still "take us as you find us" sorts of places, private domains where people — mostly blokes — could be themselves. When old houses were being remodelled along the lines of the all-electric kitchen and it was becoming the norm that each child should have a bedroom, the shed was beyond the reach of post-war consumerist modernisers.

The shed was a kind of anachronistic treasure-trove of artefacts. Here were the displaced lampshades and chests of drawers, there the enamel colanders and baking trays. Most of these collectables were invisible to the boys around the place, and it was mostly boys who'd be discovered exploring the backyard world of sheds.

But the real treasures needed no imagination.

For some reason or another, and perhaps, each for a different reason, war veterans had returned with their souvenirs. Perhaps they thought that these objects might still be required — the Korean War soon followed the war against Japan, so who knew when the next threat to Australia might arise? A well-stocked shed meant national security.

Perhaps such relics were just for jogging the memory. Few turned up inside people's houses, so they were certainly not regarded as trophies. Sharp eyes could spy atop cupboards or hanging from rafters, tin helmets, webbing, hammocks, ammunition boxes, cartridges from artillery shells awaiting conversion to serve as vases or door-stoppers, Japanese money, compasses, bits of radios and dog tags. These were all sources of wonder and triggers for wild fantasy.

The structures themselves were equally varied. Rosehill had some grand old homes, two-storeyed Victorian mansions with extensive gardens and sheds which had been stables. Some had been converted into accommodation. Others were divided into garage and laundry. All had more complicated facades than you get on the average suburban home in the 1990s.

In those days kids were not architectural critics or post-modernist deconstructers, but there was a sense in which we absorbed and appreciated the wonders of local sheds. How nostalgic we baby-boomers become as we rivet together those prefabricated boxes that now pose as garden sheds. How sad that the current deprived generation of kids cannot know that shedworld of Rosehill in the 1950s.

It explains a lot: social disintegration, families in crisis, the greenhouse effect. It seems indisputable that the world would be a better place if there were more old-style sheds. Sheds are solid. Sheds are therapeutic. Sheds can save our species. Sheds deserve respect.

Tony Smith, Forest Grove, New South Wales

Winter in Hawthorn

IN THE BEGINNING, the shed was a stable behind a mansion high on Glenferrie Hill, overlooking Melbourne, only a drop-kick from where McCubbin painted his *Winter in Hawthorn* in the 1880s.

Around about the time Hawthorn entered the VFL, in the mid 1920s, weatherboard cottages began springing up around the grand houses. In the resulting real estate carve-up, one such cottage inherited the stable in its backyard, and the Saga of the Shed began.

It began for us kids in the 1940s, when we — the family of a Victorian Railways clerk — moved into the house.

The shed had atmosphere from the beginning: big as a three-car garage, made of good timber with high exposed beams, the original wooden food bins for the horses intact, and some of the partitions still in place.

It became not only a repository for gardening utensils, tools, fire wood, and later a garage for the car, but a home away from home for four boys and their friends.

The shed's first real ornament was a German combat helmet. In 1945, as the family walked into church one Sunday morning, a digger in uniform staggered past the Immaculate Conception dragging the helmet by its chin strap. As he passed the church gates, the strength that Hitler's legions couldn't shake gave out after a night of alcohol, and he let his souvenir slip to the ground. My older brother Frankie outsprinted a flying band of novices to claim the prize.

For the next decade that German helmet with a bullet dent on the crown hung on a hook in shed, or lay on the ground, when it wasn't playing a major role in all manner of martial games. It served as the incongruous headgear of countless cowboys and indians, pirates and princes, and warded off many a green plum fired from the fork of a wicked shanghai.

And the helmet was central to our shed's darkest hour. One afternoon in the mid 1950s, as one of our running mates from up the hill, Barry Ricciardi, was sauntering home from school deciding which letter box in the street he would set fire to that evening, he had a sudden and serious call of nature. Barry lurched in our side gate, up the grassy drive and headed for the shed. There in his distress he spotted an old friend . . . an upturned German

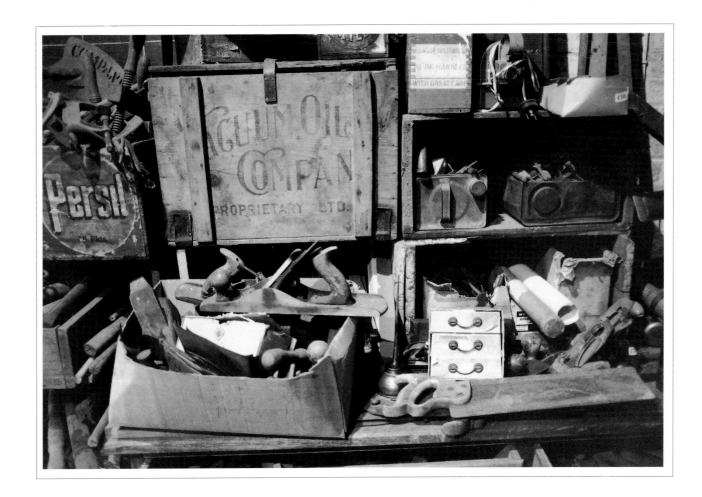

helmet. Without any malice aforethought Barry did what millions of Italians would have loved to have done as a gesture of defiance during the war. He left quietly.

The next day, while hosing the lawn, my mother happened to glance into the shed and was suddenly taken extremely poorly. Barry had confided to us boys, swearing us to secrecy; we told Mum, and Barry was banned from the premises for the rest of the summer. Mum buried the German helmet in the backyard and planted a lemon tree over it.

In the early 1930s, Mum's brother Bert jumped out a classroom window at Xavier College, Kew, and ran away to the Northern Territory. He turned up in Hawthorn again in the 1950s and moved in with us. The shed was never the same again. Bert put in a workbench, a skylight, lined one wall with tools, and built a small chookhouse in one corner. One afternoon when there was no adult presence, several of us got into the chookhouse to get feathers for an indian uprising. We left the door open and the cat killed the chooks.

Bert built a large pigeon cage to hang from a beam in the shed and Dad brought home four exotic homing pigeons and told us under no circumstances were they to be let out for a month. After three days we couldn't wait to witness our homing pigeons come home, so we let them out. They soared to the top of a large oak tree next door, had a good look around and flew off . . . to someone else's home. We escaped punishment for the death of the chooks, but we copped plenty for the disappearance of the pigeons.

Dad was superannuated out of the railways in the late 1950s, had a leg amputated, and then another. To supplement his income he worked for a starting-price bookmaker on Saturdays. The SP was always getting raided and moving to new premises. Dad offered the shed. With Bert knocking up some bush furniture, and a contact from the phone company putting in the lines, the illegal operation flourished for weeks and Mum nearly died of shame.

One Saturday, six policemen charged up the driveway towards the shed. At the same time a dozen men in shirtsleeves with pencils behind their ears, having jumped our back fence, were running down Riversdale Road. In the shed, police found a man with no legs sitting at a long table with 12 phones, all ringing. Dad was fined and the SP moved on.

With the coming of the 1960s the shed fell into disuse. Sometimes on a rainy Saturday,

Dad would sit up there drinking beer and listening to the football and Slim Whitman records at the same time, dreaming of how many Brownlow Medals he could have won if fate had dealt him a different hand.

The old stable was showing its age, and when rain started to leak onto our Morris Major, "tradesmen" were called in. It was one blistering hot day when two of Dad's mates from his pub days came to mend and paint the roof, and bitumen a path up the drive. The heat got to Jackie — he took to drinking the thinners and fell off the roof. Happy bitumened the wrong side of the drive and took Jackie to the pub, and Mum banned them both from further maintenance work.

The house was done up by yuppies in the late 1970s, a decade after we'd moved, and the shed — with its echoes of horses neighing, pigeons cooing (for a short time anyway), chooks and SPs laying, Slim Whitman yodelling, and kids yelping as they dodged flying tomahawks — was pulled down. A better fate than being turned into a playhouse for kids called Sebastian and Emily, anyway.

Tom Briggs, Glengarry, New South Wales

Death of a shed man

LEATHER
STRAP

ONE OF THE great shed men left us last week.

I have written about sheds before: how a proper shed is better than a grand hotel; and how those who manage sheds, and grow them, and coddle them through their birth and through the sparse, lonesome difficulties of adolescence, to the prime, well-cluttered years of middle life and maturity, are usually our finest citizens.

Ian MacDonald's shed was a new one to me, and I got to visit it only the once. It had cosy leather chairs and the vital organs of motorcycles polished and displayed on tidy shelves. It had several wings — it was one of those sheds which had, well, grown. Part of it had that breed of roof from which all sorts of good stuff hangs, and you could sit there and drink and tell the truth about machinery. One of its extensions sort of wrapped around the side of the house like a big warm arm, and it had a fridge full of icy cold beer perched on its elbow. Lucy, the shed-owner's daughter, in a delinquent, solicitous whisper, told me of that fridge on the day of my visit, and I applied myself with all due diligence. It was our secret fridge.

236

Partly because he was an incredibly practical man, partly because he was one of our best architects and civic thinkers, and largely because he loved motorcycles with an intense, burning passion, did MacDonald build his shed between his house and the street. That shed was the first thing you'd reach once you'd gone through his gateway. Only past the shed would you come to the back of the house.

The house faced into the block, its back to the street, so the shed gradually became the house. The yard space was mainly past the house, out in the bit we would usually call the back; fenced and private. Ian called that his front. Sometimes it filled with motorcycles too, but the easiest place to park was amongst the bushes near the street. You would gather around, beside, or in, the shed.

It's funny how you see a drinking companion on the horizon. Ian MacDonald came from an unusual direction for me — he invited me to join him and his colleagues on the Civic Trust jury, and through our numerous meetings and deliberations I revelled in his wit and wisdom and his huge concern for the look and feel of our city.

The only drink we got to share through all of that was water. But that was little matter. There would be plenty of time once the work was done. "We shall all go out to dinner," he said, and I knew we would.

So when my new mate invited me to his house for a few drinks to celebrate his eightieth birthday, I slowly filled with a calm, warm, patient anticipation.

"If you've got an old motorbike to ride, I'd advise you to bring it," he said.

The row of impacted vertebrae in my back and the various arthritic hinges and pulleys spread about my minions are reason enough for me to have long ago abandoned motorcycles as a mode of transport. Bikes have been promoted to items of pure idolatry for me: something to whisper about from a good way back; far too awesome to stroke. Leave the riding to the eighty-somethings, I told myself. I would take a taxi and, instead of thrilling transport, I would find a nice bottle.

Choosing a birth-vintage wine for an octogenarian is a difficult task — the best I could manage was a 1923 tawny. It had come from the Yalumba Museum, and had obviously been recorked and waxed with great care, so I negotiated a price, bit my lip, and headed back up the track to Ian's party.

You couldn't get in for bikes. There were dozens. Broughs and Bimmers and Vincents, Ducatis and Harley Davidsons, and one lonesome Tilbrook. Kym Bonython came in on his famous MV Agusta, and there grinning in the midst of it was MacDonald.

"Put this away," I said. "Have it later. It's special."

"Okay. I'll start working on the guest list."

He held that bottle with both hands. It was just a matter of waiting. We would be having a dinner soon, by jove.

The day prickled by — it was very hot and blue and the seedpods popped with the stubby lids. The buzz of anecdote and honeybee slowed now and then when one of the mighty old engines lit up, giving the noses as much to work on as the eyes and ears.

Ian did the rounds, but stuck mainly to his shed, where eventually, once the mobs had thinned, we sat beneath the dangling bits that would come in handy one day and pulled the corks from a few deep reds. Wendouree Shiraz at shed temperature. Australia in the summer. Lazy, bright, humorous yarns and laughter there 'neath the galvo with Pitti and Lu and some well-worn, lived-in mates. Shed gospel.

Something about Shiraz it was, too. Something about how deep and dark and compact the winesmith squashes history when he turns out a good one like the Wendouree. It was all confidence-boosting, assuring stuff. We would all last as long as that damned Wendouree.

Of course we can't.

When the bad news came, I wailed and cruised the bars, looking for the odd stray trace of this remarkable, beloved bloke with whom I would never again share communion. Then I got to thinking about that bottle of port, and took deep relish in the thought that at least he'd left with my shout warming his belly.

But no. I should have known. Ian MacDonald had promised to share that port over a dinner. At the funeral Lu said she'd found a good bottle of port she'd once bought him, and she thought there was one there from me as well. The old bloke with the scythe was among the few who had managed to force Ian to break his word. "So you'd better come and help me with it," she warned me.

You bloody bet I'll help with it. And anything else that needs to be cleaned up. And I'll never forget dear Pitti, suddenly adjusting to this foreign thing they call widowhood, looking into me to say: "It was such a short friendship, Philip". Short friendship indeed. Just a glimpse, really. A glimpse and a visit and a red in the shed. But such a bright, full, fortunate glimpse of a drinking chap on his sweet home patch. A bloke who'd actually got there.

This is no dress rehearsal, friends. This is the only chance we get.

Philip White, Adelaide, South Australia

The egg

Stamp-pad Marker for eggs.

DURING THE WAR, when the German occupation drew together what was left of our clan following bombing and imprisonments, my cousins George and Mary (Djoka and Meri for short) lived in our house. Since the local school was only intermittently operational, we had ample time for games and play. In the warm weather there were many opportunities for adventure, but winter brought the problem of getting away from the adults.

Every October, stacks of logs would appear in the back garden, their looming presence given the lie by visions of glowing stoves we knew these frosted sentinels of winter had in mind for us.

In 1942 the three of us devised, as a long-term project, a cubby-house erected between two rows of logs. As we busied ourselves with its construction, we did not know that in the years to come logs would be unobtainable and the cubby-house would not be built again.

But that winter, we luxuriated in our wooden cave. The big house was rigidly defined for us, though less by its walls than by the order that prevailed within.

By contrast, our illicit abode was an accommodating space. It might be a hospital, a school-room, a jail or a bunker which we could invade, dirty boots and all.

Much of the time, however, it was a kitchen, happily not too wholesome. Like the adults, we fantasised about food, but unlike them we were sustained, rather than thwarted, by the make-believe fare. The imaginary repasts had, at times, a realistic base in pilfered supplies: crusts of bread, onions, a carrot, a potato, old utensils, even a piece of cheese. Unfettered by rules of demeanour and reason, we created and consumed veritable feasts.

One day I stole an egg. This was a risky business as the adults knew exactly how many eggs the household had at any time and always carefully planned their deployment. Boiled, fried and scrambled eggs were not allowed; eggs were only utilised to extend and enhance staples (flour, rice, potatoes), their magic and nutrients spread thinly but fairly.

Stepping gingerly on the squishy young snow, I carried the precious egg. Dank odours of earth and mulch came up from the slush. This wafting of sweet impurities carried me happily away from the clean and frugal adult world. In the cubby, Djoka, Meri and an old tin plate awaited the egg. The cubby was enclosed on three sides by logs; thus protected from the wind, we took off our coats so that their flapping would not endanger our egg. Now we hovered and deliberated over it — just like the adults whose activities we inevitably mimicked. Finally it was decided to break the egg. It fell to 11-year-old Djoka to do so and he managed the task well, with only a little of the white spilling onto the earth floor. From its tin throne the charismatic object beckoned, luscious and gleaming, its orange dome sporting a speck of blood we knew to be the beginnings of a chicken. Such splendour was an omen of the future. As we sat dreaming, Grandfather's rubber-booted legs appeared outside the cubby-house.

The only man in the family, he was designated wood-chopper; we suspected he knew of our hide-away, though he seemed to have ignored it so far. But this time (and who knows why) he took a peek inside — and there was the egg directly in his line of vision.

Time stopped; nothing moved, though I thought I saw bits of fluff from Meri's pullover rise up in fright. Suddenly he left; the ground coughed and belched under his boots and the noise was shocking as we wondered what he would do. Most probably his grey–green eyes would turn snakey under their hooded lids as, back at the house, he hissed our names at Mother, Aunt and Grandmother.

But he returned alone. Crouching in our doorway, he spread a mat before him and knelt down on it. He was now inside, his head bent to avoid the roof. From his pockets he produced a diminutive primus and pan (mementos of soldiering in World War I). He lit the primus and put into the pan a larded spoon which he had also brought with him, wrapped in newspaper. He must have previously spotted our supplies; reaching out deftly, he salted and scrambled the egg and slid it into the pan. Fragrance of things past engulfed us and we began to relax as Grandfather placed four bits of bread around the egg. Soon it was done. Using the fork, he sliced the egg into four triangles and draped one over each piece of bread. With some ceremony, he handed out the precious morsels. We chewed slowly, just like he did. It was an emotional moment, though it was hard to say what it was we felt.

Then Grandfather said: "Time to go. Clean up later and bring back the primus tomorrow — but mind, don't light it!" And so we followed him, each virtuously carrying an armful of

Curing rabbit skins.

chopped fire wood. As we entered the house, the women nodded approvingly; unexpectedly (or was it?) Grandfather winked at us. Afterwards Djoka said it was a sign of complicity among thieves. But I thought differently; when later we sat around the kitchen stove, it suddenly struck me, for the first time, that Grandfather, too, had once been a child.

Mira Crouch, Glebe, New South Wales

Men and their sheds:
the dark side

 SOME OF MY earliest memories as a child are of playing cars and making roads in the dirt floor of my father's substantial shed complex. I recall digging up mysterious collections of small bones, no doubt small birds or chickens in retrospect, and being greatly excited by the significance of these archaeological finds. It was a vast place for a child, full of dark corners containing drums and boxes of all manner of metal objects, which I pondered over and tried to guess their possible use, and timber tools and boxes of screws and washers.

I even have dim memories of my grandfather's shed. It was dark and dingy, broken by columns of light entering through the windows overgrown with passionfruit and fractured by splinters of light driving through the cracks in the walls and roof. It smelt of dust and old engine oil and was stacked with pumpkins and rusting old tools.

The first time I came face to face with death in a shed I was a first-year intern at a large regional hospital. In our unit there had been a man, of some 50 years of age, with severe depression. He had been subjected to electro-convulsive shock treatment and all manner of drug and psychotherapy treatment. He remained significantly depressed. Although I had been playing only a marginal role in his "management", I had become quite close to him and his wife.

He was a gentle man of depth and silence.

A few days after his eventual discharge with minimal improvement, I received a call from his wife in the middle of the day. She was clearly upset and said she thought her husband may have killed himself. She had heard a shot from the shed. She was too scared to go and look and he was not answering her. She asked if I could come out to their house. I told her to ring the ambulance and I ran out of the ward, jumped in my car and tried to find the house, which was about 10 kilometres out of town. I was there about 10 minutes before the ambulance.

I cautiously wound my way through the garage to the workroom at the back. There he sat, a .22 calibre rifle at his side, blood coming out of his mouth.

He was dead.

Why had someone not asked him whether or not he had a gun? Why had the fact that he had been a prisoner of war in a concentration camp for years never been discussed?

It was a confronting experience for a young doctor, fresh out of university. It was one of the important experiences that led me to work as a family and marital therapist.

Background

When families moved from a rural subsistence or feudal system to become urban dwellers, men took up the position of being the "provider" and relegated women to the domestic domain. In so doing, men denied themselves sovereign control of their "castle".

Men believed they needed a space they could call their own, that they could control and shape to suit themselves exclusively, and this led to the birth of the humble, or at times not so humble, backyard shed. In this new domain, they retained almost total control by an exclusionary process that limited admission to a select few. While many women and children were happy with this, a few saw it as a means by which men legitimised their withdrawal from domestic, partnering and child-rearing responsibilities.

The issue of "control" is always important for men. I think that this is one area where recent culture has failed men dismally. A man has to be in control, of everything, all the time. If he is not, then there is something wrong with him. He's not a proper bloke, not a man's man. What is a man to do when he feels overwhelmed by sadness or a sense of failure or profound rejection? How is he to cope? The shed, being under his total control, is a space in which he can "take charge".

It is perhaps hard for some to appreciate the depth and significance of the relationship between the man and his shed. Should a man be separated from his shed prematurely, or unwillingly, a life-threatening withdrawal and grief reaction can occur. It can leave the man hopeless and helpless, with no sense of meaning or purpose, alienated from his family and, at times, from life in general.

Many shed widows and orphans have been created by desperate men who choose to take their own lives in their shed. I think men choose to end their lives in their shed for many reasons. A man's shed is a space that is solely his; it is his sanctuary; and he is unlikely to be interrupted in his shed. In what is a seemingly bizarre contradiction, a man's shed is thus perhaps a place where he can end his life in a place of peace, familiarity and comfort. In addition, the means are often readily available in most sheds.

This brings me to the second and equally important aspect of the dark side of sheds: the abuse of children. This is usually sexual, and affects boys and girls, children and grandchildren, within and outside their own families. In my work I have met with countless men and women whose sexual abuse first began, and most frequently took place, in the shed. Sometimes this would take torturous proportions.

These men use all sorts of tricks and tactics. Bribery and blackmail, threats, coercion and force, drugs and alcohol, in order to take out their own selfish sexual gratification on those who are vulnerable, innocent and powerless.

And once again, because of the very nature of the relationship between a man and his shed, an abusive man has little chance of being discovered in his shed. I do not blame these men, since this serves no purpose. They have often been victims themselves in the past.

However, they are certainly responsible for their choices and are thus accountable for the effects of these choices on others.

This is a seriously tragic side to the not-so-innocent shed. An abused child often suffers for the rest of his or her life, and may inadvertently pass the suffering on to the next generation, and the next and the next. An abused child suffers loss of self-esteem, self-worth and self-confidence. A profound loss of trust resulting from the betrayal of what may otherwise have been an important loving relationship. A betrayal by a person who is supposed to look after the child and have the child's best interest at heart. This is shattering for the child's development and the abuse is often buried deeply in the mind for 20 to 30 years, sometimes for ever. A child who has been abused often shows the effect without a clear recollection of the cause, wrongly assuming "it is just the way I am".

Abused children feel an enormous sense of guilt and shame, falsely believing that they are in some way responsible for their own abuse. They can feel lonely and isolated, jailed by the bars of secrecy and by the threats of trouble that usually surround the secrecy. They struggle continually to try to develop a sense of control of their own lives, trying to make sense of their often difficult relationship with themselves, their partners, their family and others. They often spend their lives trying to please others, often sexually, hoping to gain a sense of reflected self-approval or acceptance. They can suffer from depression, drug and alcohol dependence and eating disorders, often of a severe nature.

I think the shed is not an innocent bystander in suicide and child abuse. By providing a secret haven, it makes available a space where this sort of behaviour can take place. An example of what can occur when troubled men isolate themselves and try to handle their pain or perversity in silence.

This is the Dark Side of sheds.

Michael Lee, Mitcham, South Australia

Stuff

Stuff, gear, materials, supplies, stock. Junk, some people call it. This is a preoccupation of shed owners and often the source of amusement or aggravation to family members and friends. "It's a shocking mess" may be an apology or it could be a deliberately coded non-apology, i.e. *put up with it or get out*.

Having lots of stuff can be a problem. Ways of storing stuff, and the problems associated with getting rid of it, are the themes of some of our stories. Several of the stories hint at a new future for the shed-owning type of person: the computer. The virtual shed is with us now.

Jugged

IT WAS ANOTHER one of the old man's money-making ideas: to clean out backyard sheds. He said that the extra income would help keep the wolf from the door. Mum suggested he start with his own backyard shed. She said it was so cluttered with junk that she couldn't even hang her washing there on a wet day. He ignored that remark.

We were quite pleased when Dad didn't rise to Mum's suggestion. The old man was a hoarder and the backyard shed was an Aladdin's cave to my brother and me. The old man never threw out anything that might be useful or worth a bob or two in the future. There were all sorts of weird and wonderful things which served as props to our vivid imaginations. As far as we were concerned, every single item in that shed was just too good to throw away. And there was that hiding place at the back, behind a pile of harnesses and horse collars, with its escape route through a gap in the back wall. There we sometimes smoked the old man's tobacco on Sunday mornings as he slept in.

There were wagon parts and tools, bits of bicycles, three parts of an old sulky, cupboards, boxes, books — and a pile of sheet lead in one corner which we stuffed inside our rabbit skins to give them extra weight when we sold them to the skin dealer. (Later we discovered that the lead was worth a lot more than the extra weight it added to the skins.)

Dad's first customer was elderly Miss Malady, who lived in the big old house — we thought it was a mansion in those days — just up above where the low level bridge crossed the river. She lived with an older invalid brother who was rarely ever seen by neighbours or townsfolk or even by the occasional tradesmen she employed. No one dared visit Miss Malady unless they had an appointment or were invited.

She was a large, big-breasted woman who dressed formally and severely, invariably clutching a big black umbrella and a huge black leather handbag. She was seldom seen away from the house but her rare appearances somehow reminded me of a battleship in full pursuit of some unknown enemy. She was also very English and very posh.

She told the old man that she had some "grand" friends coming from the old country, a Lord and his Lady no less, and that she intended to treat them in the old English style, "with good English fare and British fellowship". And His Lordship had a fine "hautomobile" which would need to be housed in the "big shed".

The old man was to clean out the front part of the shed, leaving the rear section and the workbench alone. And the items removed from the shed were to be delivered to Ikey Towner, the "hardware purveyor" with whom she had made a "most satisfactory arrangement".

"Hardware purveyor be damned!" the old man grumbled, annoyed because he had counted on some good saleable (or useable) "trash" from Miss Malady's shed.

"Old Towner's nothing more than a rotten old second-hand dealer. She shoulda made him clean the shed out himself, the miserable old . . . !" We didn't quite catch what sort of a miserable she was because the old man's voice became a mumble as he glanced over his shoulder to see if Mum was within earshot. My brother reckoned he knew what the old man said but I didn't believe that even he would call a lady like Miss Malady a bitch!

So on the following Saturday morning, the old man and I and our old Studebaker utility went to clean out Miss Malady's huge stone shed. With its slate roof and high barred windows it somehow reminded me of those jail-house windows that I'd seen in cowboy pictures. It was a spooky place and I half expected Miss Malady's mysterious brother (some of the kids said that he was a vampire who only came out at night) to leap at us from some dark corner.

The strange smell hit us the moment that we opened up the shed. The old man reckoned that there was "something dead somewhere". He tracked the smell down to a big stone jar on the workbench.

"Must be fish bait or something, gone off!" the old man said, as he leaned over the jar and peered into it. He took a quick step backwards, holding his hand over his nose. "Bloody hell!" he expostulated. "It's a possum, I reckon, that's crawled in there and died. Rotten — putrefied it is! A wonder the maggots haven't got to it." He tossed a sugar bag over the top of the jar. "We can't work with this stinking muck here." He had me take it down to the river and I threw it in, jar and all.

Miss Malady appeared just as we finished the clean-up. She was still dressed severely and carried her handbag and umbrella, even though she was in her own backyard.

"A good job!" she said. "His Lordship would be very pleased to be able to store his hautomobile under cover. Now, I want——" she began, then stopped abruptly, staring towards the workbench. "Where is it ?" she raged, turning angrily towards the old man.

"Where's what, mum ?" the old man asked as he rolled a cigarette.

"The stone jar that was right there." She jabbed at the bench with her umbrella.

"Possum or something crawled in it and died, mum," he said. "Stunk something awful, it did. So I had the boy throw it into the river."

"Dead possum!" I was sure Miss Malady was going to explode. Her normally pallid face had turned purple and her eyes seemed to bulge. "You — you barbarian!" she howled. "It was jugged hare — jugged hare. You fool . . . jugged hare that I was especially preparing at great expense for His Lordship, to make him feel at home."

I was sure that she was going to attack the old man, and so was he. We nearly fell over each other getting out of that shed, and I beat the old man home by a good 10 minutes.

I don't know if he ever got paid for cleaning out Miss Malady's shed. I know that I never received the shilling the old man had promised me for helping. Miss Malady never spoke to the old man again, and if she saw him in the street, she would cross to the other side. And the old man would mutter fiercely about "bloody pommies eating rotten meat . . ."

And he somehow lost interest in cleaning out other people's sheds.

J.A. Kent, Port Fairy, Victoria

The inspection

SHIRLEY WAS VISITING us for the first time since she and Thea graduated from the Women's Royal Australian Army Officer Cadet School in Mildura 30 years ago. They have long since left the Army, and both miss the "spit and polish" environment.

Of course Thea wanted her home to be in "inspection order" for the visit. It was dusted spotless, furniture polished, rugs beaten, lawns mowed, gardens weeded, shrubs clipped and rubbish removed. The urge to paint a row of rocks in regimental colours was resisted. So was refurbishment of the shed.

Work areas in the shed are often covered in layers of fresh wood shavings, metal filings, sawdust, paint or plaster. Clean-up starts before the next job, but the arrival of a visitor is not — in the shed owner's jargon — a job.

Otherwise the shed is kept tidy with tools returned to the shadowboard, paint tins lined up with labels showing, oils and greases correctly stowed and so on. Special racks in the ceiling store long pieces of wood while other racks secure three ply, particle board and panels. Drawers contain nuts, bolts, nails, snaps, snails and puppy dog tails — neatly set out in rows.

Time was when people were invited to visit the shed — but that was before The Carpet. A large Persian carpet marks the spot for the family car to park. Here the shed exudes showroom splendour. The Carpet surrounds the car to form a deep rich mantle upon which the shed owner may alight on his return home. It is kept clean to highlight exquisite colours and markings.

Few people know that there is one small blemish on this otherwise priceless work of art. A small worn patch in the middle had relegated the carpet to the tip many years ago. Its rescue was a triumph for the shed owner when scavenging for something far less important. The patch is now well hidden beneath the car. The "off-limits" rule was introduced very soon after an acquaintance questioned the wisdom of carpeting a shed!

It was a splendid day for the visit. Clear blue skies allowed Thea to show off her home to the best advantage. The midday meal was excellent and time raced by. The ladies chatted

on happily, rarely out of each other's sight. It appeared that the sanctity of the shed had not been compromised.

The arrival of a brief thank-you note from Shirley a few days later confirmed that she had enjoyed the visit very much. She also revealed the depth of her early military training and her friendship, in the crisp PS at the end:

"Bill needs a new carpet in his shed!"

William P. Smith, Garran, Australian Capital Territory

Anthropologists, keep out!

ALL RIGHT. We know that a shed is a cave — a den, a cubby, a refuge for the frustrated hunter–gatherer. The mower that lives there is a fantasy war-horse. And so on. But this is Private. Keep Out. This Means You!

My present shed is a midden, an acted protest against law and order. I enter it only to toss in old newspapers, discarded clothes, empty bottles and whatever. Meaning, but not meaning, to order and recycle it all one day. One day.

But the shed of my childhood: that was a real shed. Made by a real Australian improviser without the help of a planning officer or building supplier, it was essentially eight poles of very remote provenance, clad in galvanised iron that had long lost whatever moral stature BHP had tried to train into it, and the whole draped in chicken wire and creeper.

It had no floor except for a scattering of demoralised gravel.

And if "shed" evokes the image of benches and silhouetted pegboard, you can keep out, too. My shed had furniture of an older kind. First, there was a piano case. Imagine a coffin made to bury an upright piano, its hinged lid concealed — and could go on concealing, as far as I was then concerned — some basic gardening tools, mainly a battered mattock and a distorted fork.

Then there were two tea chests, full of books which I now believe to have come out with the First Fleet, or not long after. The chests, books and all, were already sinking into the damp soil. At this distance I wonder how many eighteenth-century rarities in tree-calf bindings went to mildew and earthworms.

The nearest thing to a working surface in my shed was a retired dining table. Like the tea chests it was sinking, but faster, thanks to its sharp porcelain castors. (Do I imagine the porcelain castors? Probably. I think, indeed, that there was a ring of white mould around a thick place.) The table's surface had a patina of cuts, burns and paint drips. Like the books, the table may have had some potential value. But inside the house, where my widowed mother and her daughters lived, it was Art Deco.

Lastly, there was a Saratoga trunk. I know it was a Saratoga trunk because the cousin who brought it from the United States (by Matson Line and SA Railways) said it was a Saratoga trunk. I am probably one of the few people, therefore, equipped to describe a Saratoga trunk. Begin with a box of wood about right for two porters. Clothe it in grey canvas, reinforced with hickory battens, put cast-iron latches wherever they will go, and cast-iron knobs on all eight corners. That it is a Saratoga truck. No trouble. I do not know whether there was anything inside the Saratoga trunk. But it, too, was on its way down.

Sheds are in principle for being useful in. For three years I can remember only skulking in ours. "Skulking" meaning doing nothing much except staying out of the way of such chores as my sisters might think appropriate. (They were my sisters as well as being my mother's daughters; but they were bug-eyed monsters to the household's only male.) "Skulking", too, is a retrospective word. I thought that I was gainfully employed reading old copies of *Women's Weekly*.

Skulking, also, is something you grow out of. When most young men begin to find their bodies behaving unpredictably I discovered radio, known nowadays as electronics. Our shed became my radio shack, where I built things out of second-hand parts bought with precious pocket-money at a magical mystery shop in Pulteney Street, Adelaide. I forget what the initials mean, but I can swear that I made "hook-ups" with names like BFO and TRF, and at one time even made an illicit transmitter which made howls in the neighbours' news programs.

We all grow up. That was another age. There is a block of flats where our house was, and concrete covers the site of the shed. But I do not believe that it was ever demolished: it was simply resumed, piano case, tea chests, table, Saratoga trunk, poles, iron, creeper and all, by the mothering earth. Or so I prefer to believe …

Edgar Woods Castle, Tungkillo, South Australia

The shed geologist

IT IS NOT that there is a lack of shelf space in the shed, but I always find that because of the clutter on the workbench, I am forced to work in an area about the size of a small novel. This is not always ideal — especially when the item being worked on is the size of an encyclopaedia.

Stuff can be roughly pushed aside using the partially constructed item as a bulldozer — a process known as "making room". This in itself is fraught with danger as it can often result in upsets, breakages, and spills of tools, screws, paint and other interesting fluids.

This is where my theory of shed geology comes into play. There has evolved a sedimentary effect from the detritus and effluvia of old projects being deposited layer upon layer. These layers can be excavated, classified and dated using the techniques developed by archaeologists. Like the geological equivalent, the sedimentary layers are subject to upheaval, folding, lifting, quaking and — depending on the mix of solvents — even volcanic activity.

Meanwhile, the shelves sit bare whereas the bench groans under the gross weight of overburden. Besides causing a waste of time (are the pliers in the Cretaceous or the Jurassic period?) whole sets of goods are purchased unnecessarily. Each trip to the hardware store usually requires the purchase of cuphooks, two-inch nails, screws and glue. Once back in the shed they are placed carefully on the bench where they just sink into the mire and disappear within hours. Efforts to locate missing items are invariably futile and only raise the blood pressure.

If the items are required with any degree of urgency, the only sensible course of action is to purchase a new set. Of course on return from the store, the pre-existing set will be plainly visible — due no doubt to a sudden, natural upheaval of the bench's crust. The new and the old (screws, let's say) are placed side by side and, as a gesture towards good stock-rotation, half of the old packet is used. The one and a half packets remaining will then be swallowed before the next weekend when a mere six screws are required. Needless to say they can never be found, so yet another packet is purchased and on return from the store, the one and a half packets are mysteriously found in the green bowl on top of the kitchen fridge . . .

Obviously the only way to get on top of a problem like this is to have a good inventory of all resources. For those unfamiliar with the term, "resources" refers to tools, materials and consumables. For those unfamiliar with the term, "consumables" means nails, screws, cuphooks and glue. Resources can include previous projects (especially if only partially completed), and commercial products and components especially from bygone eras and preferably not in working order.

For those who have become confused — all the above terms can be best defined as junk. This is the most frequent word uttered by visitors.

In bygone days, inventories were usually neatly entered into a book. With the more important inventories, the book was called a ledger and was of greater dimension than most encyclopaedias.

Needless to say, I haven't room on the benchtop to devote to such a ledger so I have engaged a more modern method to solve my problem — after all, this is the age of computers. Imagine the thrill of being able to inquire of the computer: "Tell me all about the two-inch nails"; and receiving the reply: "One packet beside the blue paint, half a packet under the tinsnips and there are 12 in that saucer/ashtray — but they are all a bit bent."

Now I don't imagine for a moment that I have stumbled across anything new. I'm sure that some businesses have been using computers in their workshops for years. Mindful of the fact that computers are such expensive items, I have invested in a very old computer from a fairly old but reputable business. I did price a new machine but, given its small size, it seemed to be very poor value for money.

My computer requires that three-phase power be connected to the shed, but this is a facility I had long planned to install. It is rumoured that the glass vacuum-valves which need replacing are still being manufactured in Russia or Brazil. All that remains to be done is to clean out the paint from the sockets (perhaps the result of a little room-making or, indeed, a volcano) where the new valves will go and to locate some electrical switches from deep within the Triassic era. The computer's workshop manual stipulates that this sort of work should be performed by raising the top — but of course, the top is covered with this thick layer of clutter . . .

Michael Luxton, Red Hill, Queensland

The modern shed

Honey! Tea's ready!
OK Love. Be right there.
Just got one more thing
to grab.
His tea goes in the oven
automatically,
covered with a plate.
Sorry darl. Real good stuff.
Come in handy one day.
Delicious tea.
Bits dripping onto chin.
What is it? Meatloaf, eh?
Yeah, I love meatloaf.
So what kept you? A little tense.

Oh, a real beaut thing.
Been looking for it for ages.
Just fits, too.
More sauce dribbling.
I'd give you a hand but I'd
better get back to it.
The peace of the almost
clean kitchen is shattered
by a misery filled moan.
What's up honey?
He appears. Grey. Dishevelled.
I can't believe it. Useless, pile,
crash, boom, junk.
Single words fall incoherently

from his lips.
She wipes her hands dry
on her apron
and rushes to console him.
It's OK, honey.
Matthew's 16. He'll fix it.
Maybe it's time we threw out
a few things anyway.
They make their way back
to the scene of devastation.
Everything seemed frozen in time.
Still.
I've overloaded the hard drive
again, love. It's crashed.

Don't worry honey. We'll salvage
the important stuff. Norton's a great
doctor — compress some stuff we
may not need for a while. Maybe
even take some stuff off altogether.
He shudders at the thought,
but knew she was right.
I'll make you a cup of coffee.
You'll see. Be right as rain in no time.
Why didn't he just collect tin for
dog kennels, like his dad did,
instead of useless games, sounds and
screensavers, she mutters to herself.
Damn virtual shed!

Juniris Harrop, Ballarat, Victoria

Cleaning out the shed

BAKING POWDER CAN

BOARD

OUR SHED IS not a workshop. It's just the place where we keep the gardening gear, and where we store all those things that may come in useful again some day.

Such treasures had been piling up in there for about 10 years when our suburb was hit by a plague of rats. Our shed was an instant haven. The rats would emerge in the early evening to run along the pergola and into the vines, out of reach of our frustrated dogs. We left the shed door open, hoping the dogs would ferret out the rats. But there was too much junk.

Poison had to be the answer.

We quickly disposed of the odd carcasses in the garden, but soon a ghastly smell began to waft from the shed. The source was obviously buried under 10 years of treasures.

There was nothing for it but to *clean out the shed*.

Jim, an obliging friend with a trailer, helped us take everything out of the shed and onto the lawn. Everything truly past its use-by date went on to the trailer for the tip. At last a furry corpse was uncovered, and quickly popped into a double garbage-bag. Soon after, in a far corner, the daddy of them all, a huge fellow, very dead and obviously the main source of the terrible pong. Quickly into the bag and on to the trailer. Jim said he could smell the bag on the trailer from inside the car. And so he threw it into an old suitcase bound for the tip, and fastened the catch.

When Jim pulled up at the tip, the first thing he lifted off was the suitcase, putting it on the ground. When he turned back to lift off some of the other stuff, a fellow from a car nearby came up, grabbed the suitcase, flung it onto his back seat and took off like a rocket.

Did he think that weight was the Crown jewels?

What a surprise in store!

Jean Tainsh, Collinswood, South Australia

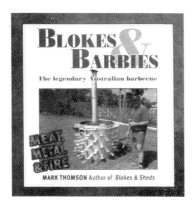

Blokes & Barbies
by Mark Thomson

In *Blokes & Barbies*, author/photographer Mark Thomson investigates this Australian legend, revealing just what it is that makes the barbie sizzle. Marvels of backyard engineering are here, along with the people behind them. Whether it's a giant dragon cooker made from recycled tools and car parts, or a shovel stuck over a few burning sticks on the ground, the result is the same – the great Aussie barbie.

It doesn't really matter if you burn the chops. The beer may even be warm, what counts is that you are building on the legend of the Australian barbecue.

ISBN 0 7322 6888 5

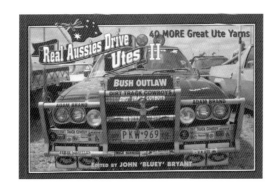

Real Aussies Drive Utes II
edited by John 'Bluey' Bryant

From the author of *Real Aussies Drive Utes* comes a new collection of funny stories involving one of Australia's most beloved icons – the ute.

You see 'em every night in TV ads; towing skiers across salt flats and working up a storm in the outback. They've got their own racing series, with big Aussie V8s going head to head on city and regional racetracks. And rural ute musters are drawing bigger crowds than ever before.

The ute and the lifestyle it represents is attracting people who, a decade ago, would never dream of owning a *commercial* vehicle. As more and more people climb aboard a ute, their destinations, experiences and adventures are becoming richer and more humorous.

This collection of 40 great ute yarns celebrates the pure essence of being an Aussie, in Australia's own invention, the *ute*.

ISBN 0 207 19963 9

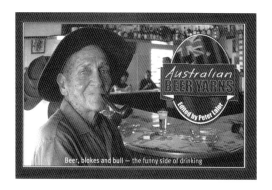

Australian Beer Yarns

edited by Peter Lalor

Why is one of our prime ministers in the *Guinness Book of Records*? How many beers did Rodney Marsh really drink? How did beer save the life of a bloke bitten by a bloody big brown snake?

The answer to these and many other burning beer-related questions can be found in the pages of the great Aussie volume, *Australian Beer Yarns*.

Peter Lalor is the beer writer for *The Daily Telegraph* — what he doesn't know about beer could be written on the back of a very small coaster. Every day at work, he's reminded of what many of us already know — beer is a subject close to almost every Australian's heart.

With this collection of funny, frank and fascinating beer stories, Peter Lalor has managed to create every beer lover's dream — the perfect book to flip through while you're enjoying a cold one.

ISBN 0 7322 7091 X

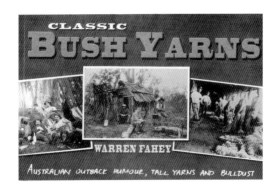

Classic Bush Yarns

by Warren Fahey

The Australian sense of humour was born of convict blood, hopeful gold diggers, itinerant bush workers, canny swagmen, iron-backed bush women, laconic soldiers, sweaty factory workers and larrikin city-slickers.

Classic Bush Yarns is a collection of the folklore which forms the basis of Australian culture and humour. Although similar to jokes, and some have had their circulation as such, yarns are quite different. They are the descendants of a tradition of storytelling that has all but disappeared. They spin a tale, drawing listeners in and inviting them to meet people like Lazy Len, Dad and Dave, and Sandy the Shearer – the characters that are keys to our past and our unique culture.

ISBN 0 7322 7048 0